Pursuing Peace

*Case Studies Exploring the Effectiveness of
Theophostic Prayer Ministry*

Fernando Garzon, Psy.D., Editor

Pursuing Peace
Case Studies Exploring the Effectiveness of Theophostic Prayer Ministry
by Fernando Garzon, Psy.D., Editor

Printed in the United States of America

ISBN 978-1-60647-202-6

www.xulonpress.com

Table of Contents

Acknowledgements vii

Editor's Note.. ix

Preface.. xi

Chapter One: Introduction: "I Didn't Know How Else to Live............................13

Chapter Two: From Marah to Elim: Karen Meets Jehovah Rapha.....................21

Chapter Three: Gloria Meets El Roi: The God Who Sees Me 39

Chapter Four: Returning Home Safely: Teresa's Journey 57

Chapter Five: Christine's "Song of Solomon" 69

Chapter Six: What Does It All Mean? 83

Chapter Seven: Common Questions Asked Concerning Theophostic Prayer
                    Ministry..97

Appendix: Sample Forms Used in the Study.....................................113

Acknowledgements

No research study gets completed without the help of a lot of people. First, we would like to thank our clients who participated in this project. They chose to explore Theophostic for themselves and we have learned much from their experience. Ed Smith and Theophostic Ministry itself were very open to our project. They cooperated fully and Mr. Smith was very receptive to our questions.

We have also depended upon the generous contributions of individuals from many churches to fund this project. In an ideal world, our research would have been grant-funded, but foundations normally don't fund preliminary studies. Without the support of interested individuals, we could not have done the testing that makes this research much better scientifically than just hearing and believing someone's story. To prevent potential bias, we also used the funds to have independent reviewers examine the research results and talk with the clients themselves. We are grateful for these reviewers taking their time to insure the results were interpreted in an unbiased way.

Several friends, colleagues, and graduate students played a part in reading over this manuscript to make sure it made sense to "everyday people" and yet also contained useful information for scientists who might be interested in studying Theophostic. You would have gotten a much more confusing manuscript without them! Finally, we are grateful to the Lord Himself for the abundant grace He has given us in all aspects of this study. Partially as a response to that grace, none of the members of the research team will receive royalties from the selling of this book.

Editor's Note

None of the authors of this book involved in this research project are affiliated with Theophostic Prayer Ministry or Dr. Ed M. Smith. This was an independent study carried out by mental health professionals and lay ministers under the leadership of Dr. Fernando Garzon. This book should also not be used to make an assessment of the Theophostic Prayer procedure. It is not written to provide the protocol or present a "how to" manual for doing or understanding Theophostic Prayer. All evaluation of the Theophostic process should be undertaken by using the 2007 TPM Basic Training Seminar Manual and other published materials provided through New Creation Publishing.

Please do not attempt this form of prayer ministry without completing the full training that is provided through New Creation Publishing (www.theophostic.com). To attempt this ministry approach without the completing the fuller training could result in unfortunate outcomes. If you desire to do this form of ministry please invest the time and energy in order to apply it correctly. This book WILL NOT equip you to do this otherwise.

Preface

In the world of counseling there are many goals and outcomes the counselor may desire for his or her counselee. However, high on most lists is the hope the client will come to know peace. Most counselors desire their clients to live life free from worry, anxiety, fear, despair, hopelessness and other disturbing emotions. How blessed it is when the counselor can ask his or her counselee how he or she is doing they can say, "I am at peace. I feel good."

The Apostle Paul wrote we should "Be anxious for nothing, but in everything by prayer and supplication with thanksgiving let your requests be made known to God. And the peace of God, which surpasses all comprehension, will guard your hearts and your minds in Christ Jesus" (Phil. 4:6-7). People in every age have either knowingly or unknowingly pursued peace. Sadly most have not sought God's peace but rather have tried to know peace through vain and futile attempts in self gratifying behavior. The peace of God is not found in selfish pursuits but in surrender and submission of one's self to God. God's peace goes beyond logic and reason and beyond the ability of any human to self-attain it. However, when it is known it settles the waves in the most tumultuous sea.

Theophostic Prayer Ministry has as its primary goal that people know the truth of God and thereby experience the "peace that surpasses comprehension" in the places that once harbored deep pain. Thousands of ministry recipients the worldwide are claiming they are finding truth and peace and that they have lasting fruit. Nevertheless, this is only personal testimony and lacks *scientific* evidence. However, even though I (Fernando) have seen good results myself using the Theophostic approach, some may suggest this could happen for a lot of reasons. The skeptic still asks the question "Does Theophostic really work or not?" He wants to see the empirical evidence to substantiate the claims of so many people who say they are finding peace. While I am asked that question a lot, I can frustrate many people with my reply. All I can say right now is "We are in a very early stage of research, and science always moves slowly."

Yuck, what an aggravating response! It's also an important one. Any spiritual or psychological intervention needs to be evaluated carefully, systematically, and slowly. Think of researchers like a turtle crossing the road. It takes a while to cross and a car at the wrong time (bad research findings) could ruin everything.

Indeed, we scientists systematically gather much information before we give a clear-cut answer about anything. In some ways, we're even distant cousins to politicians. We hedge our bets, dodge and weave, and even define words in an amazingly unusual fashion. "Ugh!" you might say. We all hate it when politicians appear to be hedging, but researchers do so for a very different reason. We're not waiting for the poll numbers to tell us what opinion to give; we're waiting for solid data from expensive, well-designed studies that have been repeated several times.

So what can we say as researchers currently in regards to Theophostic? We have heard many reports from a lot of people. We've also heard about a few bad experiences, too. It is important that we discover if the good outcomes are indeed a result of Theophostic Prayer and also we must determine if the bad reports were an outcome of genuine TPM or just simply bad therapy called TPM when in fact it was not. Research can help us find this out.

Most reports, positive or negative, are called "anecdotal evidence," which is another way of saying they are someone's story, but there's no objective testing to verify the story. That's why we did this outcomes-based case study research. It's a first small step along the way of investigating Theophostic Prayer.

Since we know people from a variety of backgrounds are interested in Theophostic, we've endeavored to write this project's findings in such a way that nonscientifically-trained readers should be able to understand it. The cases are framed as stories by the clinicians involved in treatment. The testing numbers for each case will speak for themselves. You won't have to be a rocket scientist to look at the scores to determine whether these people were helped. As such, this research is much more reliable than just counting on someone's story alone. We'll follow the individual cases with a summary of all the study's findings so you can see how the group looks as a whole, again, letting the numbers speak for themselves. Sometimes we'll sound like politicians again, hedging our bets by noting the limitations to the research method employed. Remember, this is only a start.

We also interviewed Ed Smith to answer common questions asked about the Theophostic process. This interview is found in the final section of this book. Finally, we'll indicate where the research needs to go from here to answer that one "simple" question of whether Theophostic works. May the Lord bless you in what follows.

Chapter 1: Introduction

"I Didn't Know How Else to Live"[1]

Since the autumn of 1981, I had been consumed with bulimia. For 21 years—my entire adult life—my every waking moment was focused on looking for opportunities to binge and purge, planning the binges, bingeing, purging, cleaning up, covering up, over and over, ad nauseum (pun intended). I told a network of lies too intertwined to keep straight. Bulimia took over every aspect of my life; it permeated every corner of my mind. I shoplifted, stole from my husband and children, charged thousands of dollars on credit cards—whatever it took—to be able to binge and purge.

Especially because I was a Christian, I felt incredible shame. My husband loved me, and I was a mother of six children. In my moments of clarity, I would look around me, see my husband, children, all the trappings of the "good life", and wonder why I seemed willing to throw it all away.

I had sought help from every source I ever heard of: Three 30-day stays at in-patient psychiatric treatment centers, five different antidepressants, a stream of counselors (cognitive therapy, psychoanalysis, hypnosis, behavior modification, endless self-help books, pastoral counselors), numerous prayer and deliverance sessions, and anything else I could find. It would always end up the same. I would embrace the program, often with a sense of renewed hope, determined to make it work. But inevitably, without exception, I would eventually find myself back in the "pig sty", continuing in my old self-destructive pattern. I would achieve varying periods of "recovery" (meaning I could abstain, with great effort, from bingeing and purging, but it was a constant mental battle), from a few days, to a year or more, but each "recovery" ended with a crash of defeat, perpetuating my shame, leaving me with a burden of hopelessness. Each therapist would grow frustrated with my lack of success and eventually they or I gave up.

My family and my faith were the only things that kept me from ending it all. I was a burden to my friends, no one could help me, and I had drained my family of all its financial resources. There was no way out.

One day in my women's Bible study, I started hearing some of my friends talking about a therapist that was using a unique prayer approach that they said was helping them with their own problems. Some of them had struggles as bad as mine, so I listened intently. "Joan, go see her," they encouraged me, "You've tried everything else. What can it hurt?" Flickers of hope surfaced despite the layers of discouragement and fear from previous failures. Finally their prodding won out. I made an appointment.

Since I knew the first thing the therapist would ask me to do was to get a medical evaluation (something very important for those who struggle with Bulimia, by the way), I did it before I called to schedule the first appointment. When I did call, the counselor answered the phone, listened to my pain, and made an appointment for two days later. I asked her what kind of praying she did, because I was sure I'd been exposed to every type of counseling and inner healing prayers in existence. She said, "Through prayer I help you to come into the Lord's presence, you make the choice to feel the pain in your life and connect to its lie-based source, you expose this false belief to the Lord and He replaces it with His Truth. The outcome is freedom and peace" She then asked me to prepare a list of all the reasons why I thought I continued to binge and purge and bring it to the first session.

That wasn't hard. I came up with a 2-page list, which I brought to the initial appointment. None of it was a revelation to me, but it was amazing to see all of these "reasons" together. The counselor then asked me, "Which of these reasons seems to be the strongest, most compelling reason that keeps you in this pattern?"

I replied: "If I don't binge and purge, the terrible deprivation I feel may destroy me." She then prayed that the enemy would not interfere with what the Holy Spirit wanted to do during our time together. I closed my eyes. She asked me to focus on the thought that if I didn't binge and purge, the deprivation would destroy me; she asked me to allow the feelings to grow, and to describe what I was experiencing mentally, emotionally, and even physically.

As she asked me this, I felt panicky. More than that, I felt fearful, desperate, anxious, helpless, even terrified. My stomach felt as if it was in knots, my face frowned up, and I clasped my hands tightly together. She asked me to continue to focus on my discomfort and asked me if I was willing to connect to the place where this panicky-fearful-anxious feeling first came to me. She encouraged me to remember and know that I could trust God wanted to speak to me. I was just to report any thought, feeling, sensation, impression, words or ideas that occurred to me, and to trust Him to interpret.

I waited in silence as she prayed. At first I had nothing to report, except that the anxiety was still strong. After a few moments a memory came to mind. I had a distinct image of myself, like I was five years old. My brother (then seven) was with me, and we were both sitting in the living room floor playing, but tired and hungry.

"This is strange," I told my therapist, "I haven't thought about this incident for a long time. I even feel like a little needy kid!" She encouraged me to permit any feelings that arise and to explore the sense of neediness.

"Why do you feel needy?" she asked.

"I'm hungry. Both my parents worked and James and I were often alone until they got home." The tears were now streaming.

"How do you feel in this hungry, alone state?"

"Hopeless. If I don't eat I'll die. No one cares for me." I paused as I realized another aspect. "Funny, I also feel ugly and bad. My brother used to tease me a lot when mom and dad weren't home. I remember that, too."

Carefully, my therapist listened and explored this painful memory with me. It wasn't a new one for me. I'd talked about some of these times in other therapies many times before, only now the feelings were full force inside of me, like they had never really left me.

"Joan, I'm going to read back these beliefs I've heard you saying. Allow the feelings to surface as I read." Calmly, my therapist began. "I'm alone. No one will care for me. I'm ugly.

If I don't eat, I'll die." Agony, shame, and hopelessness gripped me. She then asked, "Are you willing to hold these beliefs up to the Lord and allow Him to reveal His truth to you about them?" I agreed. Then she prayed, "Lord Jesus, what is Your truth to Joan about these beliefs? Would you reveal this truth in whatever way you see fit?"

What happened next I can't quite describe. It was like a warm bright light filled the living room. I saw Jesus in the room with us [Editor's note: It is understood that people do not see Jesus in the flesh during a ministry session, but rather a Holy Spirit created word picture representing the presence of Christ. It is also understood that many people may never have an visual images in a session. God is free to deal with people in any form that He chooses.] I saw Him walked over to me and picked me up. I've never felt so comforted in all my life. Quietly, He whispered in my ear, "I will never leave you or forsake you." Somehow, I knew it was all right. Somehow, that empty void began to be filled.

My therapist sat quietly while Jesus (the Holy Spirit) ministered to me. The tears that were once of sadness now changed to deep, glowing joy. I was filled.

I left that appointment feeling different, in a way I couldn't explain. I didn't even want to analyze it. I felt as if I were being carried. I had been bingeing & purging out of control for weeks, months and years before this day. The next day, I awoke, still feeling carried, and had no desire to binge and purge (although I had the opportunity to do so).

I continued the counseling appointments for the next few weeks. Each time, I discovered more lies and the Holy Spirit gently replaced them with His truth. Day after day, I found myself not bingeing and purging, and not even thinking about it. I didn't even feel the slightest desire to do so! As more and more lies were replaced with truth (at a spirit level, not just a head level), my faith grew, slowly and surely. Soon, I felt a strong desire to go back to church where I shared my healing with excitement. I wanted to read the Bible, to pray, to worship, to praise the Lord, and to be closer to my husband and children. In short, I actually was having life between meals!

Soon, I knew Jesus had completely and permanently set me free from the bondage of bulimia. I also knew that He would be faithful to continue to set me free from other lies that affected me, and that He would renew my mind for the rest of my life. I was thrilled, excited, blessed beyond belief! After all the years of suffering, of others suffering because of me, of countless people praying on my behalf, of living a life consumed by sin, I was free.

For over two years now, I have been completely free from bulimia—all of it: the behavior, the thoughts, and the feelings associated with it. I have gained and maintained an appropriately healthy weight (I have even enjoyed a healthy pregnancy). I eat when I am hungry, I eat whatever I desire, and I easily stop when I am satisfied. I have had no temptations to binge or purge. Even more, if the memory of the behavior rises, it "feels" absurd, and unattached to me. It is no longer my identity. I have absolutely no fear of relapse—my healing is not dependent upon me—He who set me free is keeping me free, with no self-maintenance required! Hallelujah!

Too Good to Be True?

Some of you are filled with hope after reading Joan's testimony; others are skeptical. Perhaps some are even dismissing. Our own reaction as researchers was one of curiosity. Stories like the above are common in Theophostic circles. Are they true? Are they fabrications? Are they merely a placebo effect? Whatever your initial opinion, you are not alone. Though Theophostic

Prayer Ministry is highly praised by thousands all around the world there are some individuals who bring strong criticism against it. While testimonies can be compelling, one must ask whether "the numbers" back up the stories.

That is where this research team comes in. Who is right regarding Theophostic Prayer Ministry? Are both right? Under what conditions? As clinicians and researchers, we wanted to know. In particular, we wondered whether psychological tests and independent evaluations would support or refute testimonies like the one you just heard. As noted in the Preface, we are in an early stage of this discussion. Indeed, if you have a condition like Joan's, we are not advocating that you leave therapy and stop taking any prescribed medications!

For two years, my research team has collected data from a variety of people experiencing Theophostic Prayer Ministry (TPM). These people were having problems such as depression, anxiety, body image difficulties, and sexual abuse concerns. We administered a variety of tests and, when each case was completed, an independent clinician interviewed each client. This clinician did not use TPM and did not know what type of treatment the clients had received. Such an interview, combined with the testing, would help us determine whether the subjects in our study actually improved. This would lead to the first small step in determining what the impact of TPM actually is.

What Is Theophostic Prayer Ministry?

After reading Joan's testimony, you might want a better picture of what TPM is. Theophostic Prayer Ministry represents a type of prayer that is intended to help a client process emotionally painful memories. The harmful lie-based beliefs embedded in these memories are thought to influence the client's present condition. For example, Joan believed "If I don't eat, I'll die" and "I'm alone." These core beliefs, called "lies," may be thought of as unbiblical beliefs that go against God's revealed identity for His children found in Scripture. Ed Smith, Theophostic Prayer Ministry's founder, believes that lie-based thinking frequently maintains a person's emotional distress when non-organic conditions are involved. To deal with lie-based thinking, one must, with the Holy Spirit's grace, go to the "source and origin" of the lie and in that place receive God's truth.

A typical session may look somewhat similar to Joan's testimony that you just read. First, the prayer minister encourages the person get in touch with the emotional pain he or she is experiencing. Then, the prayer minister encourages the person to choose to connect with the source and origin of the pain. Often, one or more painful memories surface at this point. Here, the facilitator helps the person to identify the lie-based beliefs and the therapist/facilitator asks Jesus (the Holy Spirit) to reveal His truth to the person in whatever way He chooses. A nondirective style is used, and the prayer minister processes the experience closely with the person to make sure what is being sensed as coming from God actually lines up with the Bible and the character of Jesus. Ideally, the prayer continues until the client has a sense of perfect peace when experiencing the memories that surfaced. Smith's training materials detail a variety of blockages that can impede the person from receiving a healing word from the Lord and Smith also has strategies for how to deal with these.

Of course, this description you are reading is merely a brief overview. Please do not attempt this process without the full training. There are all manner of potential complications that where not addressed in this short discussion. See Smith's website (**www.theophostic.com**) for further information on the prayer form, up-to-date resources, and minimum competency requirements in order to practice it. Smith warns TPM prayer ministers not to use New Age theology/techniques, hypnosis, or guided imagery. As a matter of fact, Smith is often quoted as saying, "If a ministry facilitator ever does anything to move the session in any direction that he thinks it should go then he is no longer doing Theophostic Prayer." The reader would benefit reading the summary description of a ministry session found in the *Ministry Session Guidelines* found on the TPM website.

What is this Case Study Research?

Now that you've read a testimony about TPM and understand what the approach entails, we can describe the research design better to you. First, let's consider who did the TPM with the people in our study. We wanted to make sure the TPM practitioners truly represented what happens when this prayer form is properly administered, so we selected licensed mental health professionals who had been trained through the training that Ed Smith provides and lay counselors who had attained a high level of experience in the approach.[2] The professionals worked with clients typical of regular outpatient psychotherapy—persons suffering from anxiety, depression, etc., and the lay counselors worked with clients typical of church prayer ministry centers. These lay counselors were also under the direct supervision of a licensed mental health professional.

Each client was given psychological and spiritual tests after every 10 hours of treatment. At the end of treatment, each received a half an hour interview with a professional who does not use TPM and was not affiliated with the study. This was an important component of the research, since each of us on the research team previously had seen very good results using TPM. Such familiarity could have potentially biased our interpretations of the study's data. This situation is not uncommon amongst most researchers studying other techniques in counseling as well. For instance, cognitive therapy clinicians who have had good experiences with cognitive therapy often research cognitive therapy, behavioral therapists with good experiences with behavioral therapy often research behavior therapy, etc. This is especially true at the early stages of research, since no one else often is interested enough to begin researching an approach otherwise. An objective outside reviewer therefore helps researchers in these instances get an unbiased review of whether participants actually improved or not. Following the post-treatment interview and testing, the tests were again administered three months later. This helped us determine whether the improvements "stuck."

The tests given included the Symptom Checklist 90R[3], the Dysfunctional Attitude Scale[4], the Spiritual Well-Being Scale[5], and the Religious Orientation Scale-Revised.[6] At ten hour intervals, the end of treatment, and three months later, clients completed these tests. The therapists and lay counselors also completed rating scales at these intervals to give their own impressions of how the clients were doing. Clients also completed some satisfaction surveys at the end of treatment and three months later (See Appendix). A couple of summary tables will help you learn more about the testing instruments we used. Table One briefly describes the subscales of the Symptom Checklist 90R. Table Two describes the Dysfunctional Attitude Scale, the Spiritual Well-Being Scale, the Religious Orientation Scale-Revised, and other testing strategies that were used.

SCL-90-R Scales[7]

Scales	Brief Description
Global Severity Index (GSI)	Measures the overall level of emotional distress. It is a very key overall summary scale for the SCL 90R.[8]
Somatization	Focuses on concerns about physical health and bodily pains.
Obsessive-Compulsive	Reflects struggles with unwanted thoughts or impulses, as well as the need to perform ritualistic actions to assuage these thoughts/impulses
Interpersonal Sensitivity	High scores suggest self doubt, feelings of inadequacy, and a sense of inferiority that lead to overly sensitive reactions to others.
Depression	Measures symptoms common in clinical depression.
Anxiety	Focuses on symptoms common in general anxiety and also panic attacks.
Hostility	Reflects thoughts, feelings, and actions common to people experiencing anger and resentment.
Phobic Anxiety	Measures symptoms seen in most persons who suffer from a phobia.
Paranoid ideation	Reflects the amount of mistrust and suspiciousness seen in relationships. High scores can sometimes indicate paranoia and potential paranoid delusions.
Psychoticism	This scale appears poorly named since it measures a full continuum from mild interpersonal alienation to true psychosis. Withdrawal, isolation, peculiar thoughts, and true psychosis (at higher levels) are included in this subscale.

Other Measures Used

Dysfunctional Attitude Scale[8]

Measures harmful beliefs that are common when one is experiencing depression symptoms. Higher scores reflect more dysfunctional thinking. Since TPM claims to reduce lie-based thinking, we included this measure. Over the course of therapy, scores should decrease if TPM is helping in this area.

Spiritual Well-Being Scale[9]

Focuses on a person's sense of healthy connection to God and other people. Higher scores on the total score suggest greater well-being. If TPM improves a client's spiritual functioning, scores should increase from pre-treatment to post-treatment.

Religious Orientation Scale-Revised[10]

Evaluates two types of religious motivation, intrinsic and extrinsic. High scores on intrinsic motivation reflect motivation to pursue religious activities primarily for spiritual growth reasons, while high scores on extrinsic motivation reflect other motives (desire for social support, etc.). We wondered whether TPM might increase intrinsic motivation and decrease extrinsic motivation over the course of successful treatment.

Brief Psychiatric Rating Scale[11]

The therapist or lay counselor completes this rating scale instead of the client. It indicates the progress they believe the client is making in regards to symptom levels. Over time scores should decrease if the client is improving.

TPM Client Satisfaction

How did clients themselves evaluate their progress from treatment? Questions were given at post-treatment and the 3-month follow-up. These follow-up questionnaires can be found in the Appendix.

Independent Reviewer

An unbiased opinion is important in case study research. At the end of treatment, a licensed mental health professional who does not use TPM interviewed the client to give impressions on the therapy outcome. The reviewer did not know

TPM was the treatment used. The Independent Reviewer Form may be found in Appendix.

All the cases that follow are of actual people who have experienced Theophostic Prayer Ministry. The stories were written primarily by the treating TPM practitioner(s) and express their views. Certain client informational details were changed to protect their identity. May the Lord bless you as you read the stories of Gloria, Karen, Teresa, and Christine, review the overall study findings, and hear Ed Smith's thoughts on TPM.

Chapter 1 References

1. This case is a composite combining two experiences with TPM that we've heard of. One of these was from a testimony published in the Journal of the International Association of Theophostic Prayer Ministry, volume 1, pp.5-8. Used with permission of Ed Smith and IATM.
2. To be involved in the study, the licensed therapists and lay counselors both had to have a minimum of the following: Attendance at a Basic Training seminar (including reading the basic training manual, viewing all the videos, and seeing a demonstration of TPM), at least 100 hours of previous experience administering TPM, attending an Advanced Training Seminar, and attendance at a weeklong Level One Apprenticeship training seminar taught by Ed Smith. Lay counselors also had to be supervised by licensed clinicians.
3. Derogatis, L.R. (1994). *SCL-90-R administration, scoring, and procedures manual.* Minneapolis, MN: National Computer Systems.
4. Weissman, A. N. & Beck, A. T. (1978). *Development and validation of the Dysfunctional Attitudes Scale: A preliminary investigation.* (Paper presented at the annual meeting of the Educational Research Association, Toronto, Ontario, Canada)
5. Paloutzian, R. & Ellison, C. (1982). Loneliness, spiritual well-being and quality of life. In Peplau, L. A., & Perlman, D. (Eds.), *Loneliness: A sourcebook of current theory, research and therapy* (pp. 224-237). New York: Wiley Interscience.
6. Gorsuch, R. & McPherson, S. (1989). Intrinsic/Extrinsic measurement: I/E-revised and single-item scales. *Journal for the Scientific Study of Religion, 28,* 348-354.
7. Derogatis, L.R. (1994). *SCL-90-R administration, scoring, and procedures manual.* Minneapolis, MN: National Computer Systems.
8. Weissman, A. N. & Beck, A. T. (1978). *Development and validation of the Dysfunctional Attitudes Scale: A preliminary investigation.* (Paper presented at the annual meeting of the Educational Research Association, Toronto, Ontario, Canada)
9. Paloutzian, R. & Ellison, C. (1982). Loneliness, spiritual well-being and quality of life. In Peplau, L. A., & Perlman, D. (Eds.), *Loneliness: A sourcebook of current theory, research and therapy* (pp. 224-237). New York: Wiley Interscience.
10. Gorsuch, R. & McPherson, S. (1989). Intrinsic/Extrinsic measurement: I/E-revised and single-item scales. *Journal for the Scientific Study of Religion, 28,* 348-354.
11. Fisher, J., & Corcoran, K. (Eds.), (1994). *Measures for clinical practice* (Vol. 2, 2nd edition) New York: The Free Press.

Chapter 2
From Marah to Elim:

Karen Meets Jehovah Rapha (the God who Heals)

Terry E. Zuehlke, Ph.D., L.P., & Fernando Garzon, Psy.D.

Karen was in trouble. She had recently started becoming abusive to her husband (Tom) after six months of marriage. Not willing to put up with this or to harm her, Tom and two of my former clients had insisted that she seek help. But Karen had other problems besides her temper. Karen was obsessed with food and her body image as well.

"I know I need to be here, but it probably won't change me," Karen sighed. She was a discouraged "therapy expert," which means she had gone to many professionals in the past but had always left their treatment feeling unsatisfied. True to her previous experiences, she displayed much skill in describing her condition. "I have lots of shame and guilt, a negative body image, compulsive eating, and anger [issues]...I have to have control and get my way." Yes, Karen had seen it all before, but past treatment had left her drinking only bitter waters. Hmmm, bitter waters...let's start there.

The Bible has a story of the Israelites experiencing such waters in Exodus 15:22-27. Soon after the spiritual high created when the Egyptians were drowned in the Red Sea, the people of Israel began to thirst and complain as they traveled through the wilderness. They lost the mountaintop of spiritual victory and were frustrated with their circumstances. They even began to argue that they would have been better off in the brick pits of Egypt. Tension, discouragement, and doubt filled the camp. They arrived at a place called Marah , which they believed would provide them with water. However, the waters at Marah were bitter, so the children of Israel could not drink therein. The people "grumbled against Moses" (v. 24). The place they thought would provide relief had failed to do so. Moses cried out to the Lord in this desperate situation. In response, God provided a way for the water to become sweet. At last the people's thirst was quenched, and they met the the Lord in a different way. "Jehovah Rapha" (I am the Lord who heals you.) took them from their bitterness and complaining, and gave them sweet water. He then led them to Elim, a place with twelve springs of fresh water and seventy date palms. Would I have something to offer Karen that would change her bitter waters to sweet? Could Jehovah Rapha take Karen from her life in "Marah" to her own "Elim"?

Karen's Story

Karen's story gave clues to current behaviors. Her father was an alcoholic and frequently was absent from the home. His absence actually was a hidden blessing though, because when he was present, he was often verbally and physically abusive toward Karen's mother. "He yelled all the time…You don't mess with my dad."

Karen felt distant from her mother, who was an attractive, codependent, non-nurturing woman that seemed to favor Karen's older sister. Karen herself idolized her older sister as well and felt that both her mother and sister were much prettier than she was. I marveled as I heard Karen put down her own appearance, as she was an attractive woman. She just couldn't see it.

Karen's family were non-believers; however, through a friend, she went to church and became a Christian at the age of eight. She currently attends an evangelical church, worships regularly, and has consistent devotions. Her father's continued drinking and violence eventually resulted in a divorce between her parents after 30 years of marriage, which she described as "devastating".

Prior to her own marriage, Karen and Tom had gone through extensive premarital counseling and workshops, so Karen was sure they wouldn't have the problems most people face… until this. Karen had a high school degree and worked as a retail salesperson. Tom operated his own small manufacturing company. This was the first marriage for each of them and they had no children.

Assessment of Karen's Problem

You might ask how I (Terry) was conceptualizing Karen's problem. While possessing a bubbly personality most of the time, Karen would experience lack of attention/affirmation as a signal of potential abandonment. She then would attempt to control this fear by intimidating others with angry outbursts. Today, her irritability toward others reflects yesterday's unfinished business toward both her parents. She medicated her inner loneliness with food. This approach, like the angry outbursts, came with a steep price however. The more she comforted herself with food, the less physically attractive she felt. Karen exercised vigorously to hide her over-eating. Shame became a major emotional stronghold.

In essence, Karen knew inside that she was at Marah. Her strategies weren't working and she was growing hopeless about her endless journeys through psychotherapy. Her outbursts and fleeting self-comfort through overeating and excessive exercise only hid her deep insecurities from others, but not herself. All of these were her vain attempts to get the validation she was looking for.

Some therapists might enjoy seeing my original treatment plan for Karen, so I've placed it below. Others of you may want to skip this section.

INDIVIDUAL TREATMENT PLAN

Client Name: Karen Smith   Date of Birth: 12/11/63

Subscriber Name: Same   Health Plan Name: LXLX

Presenting Problem: Hx temper tantrums "to control and get my way." "I've just been existing for years." Marital conflict, depression and anxiety.

I.   DSM-IV (5 AXIS)

Axis I: Anxiety NOS (300.0); Bulimia non-purging type w exercise (provisional) (307.51); Intermittent Explosive Disorder (312.34); Spiritual Conflicts (V62.89)

Axis II: Originally Deferred (799.9) [Dependent Personality Features noted later in treatment]

Axis III: None

Axis IV: Type(s)   Primary support group, social environment, occupation

              Severity: Moderately severe

Axis V: Current GAF: 62   Highest GAF past year: 66

II. PRESENT SYMPTOMS SUPPORTING DIAGNOSIS

Significant shame and guilt; negative body image; compulsive eating and exercise; frustration and anger; feelings of depression. "I always try to make everything positive."

III. RELEVANT FAMILY AND SOCIAL HISTORY

Youngest of three children. Father was an alcoholic who was often away from home. He was verbally and physically abusive and divorced her mother after 30 years of marriage. Mother was an attractive, non-nurturing "co-dependent" person who was often in a "bad" mood. Older sister was idolized by Karen.

IV. PREVIOUS MENTAL HEALTH SERVICES   Consulted: Y/N N/A

15 years ago secondary to Alanon involvement; other therapy experiences since

V. CURRENT IMPAIRMENTS ATTRIBUTABLE TO DIAGNOSIS

Labile and dysphoric mood; marital conflict; addictive personality features; spiritual conflicts

VI. SPIRITUAL HISTORY

Born-again believer age 8; attends evangelical church; family non-believers; worships regularly; consistent devotions.

Modalities: Individual, possibly conjoint
Medications: (name, dosage)   None
Prescribing Physician: N/A   Consulted: N/A
Duration/Frequency: Weekly sessions of 2-hour duration whenever possible

TREATMENT PROCEDURES	
GOALS RELATIVE TO IMPAIRMENTS	**OBJECTIVE CRITERIA FOR DISCHARGE**
I. Compulsions/Obsessions Diminish perfectionism about tasks; resolve key life conflicts causing negative behavior patterns; report cessation of fears; conduct life from a faith in God perspective.	1. Increase relational desires while reducing performance-based self-worth. 2. Demonstrate ability to use positive self-talk as coping strategy to abate obsessions. 3. Complete Freedom Appointment Step 2: Deception vs. Truth. 4. State integrated sense of self; rely on Christ as only defense needed.
II. Labile/Dysphoric Mood Learn to recognize excessive worry problems and to deal with them. Learn effective communication skills for positive coping results and to limit discussions about worries. Reduce the frequency of critical, angry expressions that are related to general state of depression.	1. Verbally identify the triggers and symptoms of worry using CBT with Spiritual focus. 2. Work with spouse to learn his perspective on her anxiety problems. 3. Schedule anxiety-reducing activities that can be done with and without her spouse. 4. Communicate awareness of relationship between expressions of anger and feelings of hurt that lie buried in early memories.
III. Marital Conflict Reduce conflict, hurt, doubt, and angry feelings between partners.	1. Report increased comfort with sexual contact with spouse. 2. Demonstrate increased trust in God as the healer of all traumas. 3. Identify lies / misbeliefs in historical memories and replace with the truth (Theophostic Ministry). 4. Use speaker / listener technique for conflict management. 5. Complete Freedom Appointment Step 6: Bondage vs. Freedom.

Therapist   TEZ   **Date:** 10/01/01
Client   Karen Smith   **Date:** 10/01/01

Karen's Treatment

While my educational background gave me a good framework to understand Karen's situation, it was clear the standard tools of my trade had not worked for her in the past. In short, I knew that the same old treatment strategies Karen had seen before would probably produce the same old results. Something had to be done differently this time, so I chose to use Theophostic Prayer Ministry (TPM). I explained the research project to Karen and she willingly agreed to participate. During the first three intake sessions the principles and treatment methodology of TPM were explained. Before TPM sessions commenced she listened to Dr. Smith's Introductory Tape on the ministry, and we had a joint session with her husband.

Early Treatment Challenges

The joint session with Tom was informative. More came out about Karen's needs for affirmation, her critical nature, and her belief that he found her physically unattractive. Tom spoke at length about how demanding and controlling he felt she was in the marriage. "I get accused of not thinking positively about her and she's so threatened about losing me. Without physical affirmation she feels rejected, but I'm feeling controlled."

Karen was seeing her husband as the source of her explosive outbursts. She noted, "I doubt his real feelings unless I hear them out loud. Even then I doubt [them]....I get angry to try to control him and make him listen to me. I've got to overpower him to keep him. I have such insecurities about my own body image."

At this point, Karen confirmed that she was afraid of a divorce. Tom replied truthfully that he had the resources and emotional strength to leave the marriage if it came to that. He stated however that he was willing to see if Karen's treatment with me would make a difference, and that he was glad to be involved should I call upon him later. I was encouraged by his response. Sometimes in situations like these, marital consultations and co-treatment can be as important as individual.

TPM commenced at the fourth session. I find it useful to do TPM in a double-session format when the situation allows for such. Accordingly, Karen's therapy consisted of 30 hours of psychotherapy in 19 sessions (11 two hour sessions and eight one hour sessions. One one-hour session included her husband.) The 11 two-hour sessions of psychotherapy involved TPM.

I explained to Karen that I think people come to therapy with two questions, which they may or may not realize. Typically, foremost on their minds is the question, "What are you going to give me to help me?" This kind of thinking represents the traditional "medical model" in which the doctor and his expertise are the source of your healing. Most people want to hear, "Take two of these a day for the next ten days and you should be okay." Lasting healing does not work that way. The second question, although less clearly understood or realized is, "Why do I have this problem in the first place?" I pointed out to Karen that the second question is the more important one. It pertains to the roots of the issue. I said, "If we simply address <u>what</u> to do about your concerns and avoid <u>why</u> you have them in the first place, we will be doing band-aid psychotherapy. It's like telling me you are going to save $200 this summer by controlling the dandelions in your yard by mowing your grass instead of using a lawn treatment service. That will look like it works and your yard will look as green as mine and it will look like you were smart and saved yourself some money. But, if you miss a mowing for some reason, guess what is going to be back? The weeds will be back because you focused on dealing with the fruit of the problem instead of the root of the problem." Karen agreed with this analogy. Read on and you will see how God revealed Himself as Jehovah Rapha, the God who would provide Karen with the inner healing she needed, and lead her to Elim.

The first eight hours of TPM treatment were trying for me. We were not getting break-through moments of the Lord revealing healing truth; however, the origins of Karen's presenting complaints were emerging often as the Lord brought memory after memory to the surface related to her dysfunctional family environment.

At the end of these early prayer times, Karen sometimes said she was surprised by the intensity of the session. "In the beginning [of this session]...I didn't think we were going to get anywhere. But we sure did!...This is just wild how this works. It's God, I know. But, how does this work? Am I supposed to pull the lie and the truth together? Or, do you help me piece it together?"

My response to Karen's question was very important. Karen was an "analyzer". If I told her that she and I would examine the memories, identify the lies, and do the lie-restructuring ourselves, this would have been typical of some cognitive therapy strategies of processing painful emotional memories, but it would also fit nicely with her need to always be in control. Similar to her previous therapy experiences, great insights likely would have emerged, with little real change. Instead, I told her, "Karen, our job is to 'let go and let God'....We don't want to analyze and decipher because that would be leaning on our own understanding. The whole idea is just to release ourselves and be there to listen."

Karen understood, but also acknowledged the difficulty in waiting for the Lord's truth. 'This is really hard. It's like a nightmare to believe that my mom didn't really want me." My comfort and encouragement helped her endure that pain until the Lord did speak in later sessions.

End-of-Prayer Processing Time

Karen's above comment highlights the importance of a supportive, caring relationship in TPM. Facing our pain is never easy. I took the time after each prayer to explore Karen's experience about the feelings and memories that had surfaced. What was it like for her to feel these emotions so strongly? I had to give Karen the opportunity to vent any feelings. Gently, I would listen, empathize, and encourage her to stay with the process. Such post-prayer discussion helped her stay connected with someone who cared in that "middle-state" before the Lord began speaking His healing truths. The processing also helped me to note any guardian lies around experiencing strong painful emotions that we might process in future TPM sessions.

During this time of waiting for the Lord to reveal truth, Karen continued having some significant altercations with Tom. On one occasion, she threw a pillow at him, bit him, pulled his hair, and punched him on the arm. "I still try to control him to stop his criticism," she noted.

I must admit that after these four two-hour sessions, I was getting impatient. As a professional clinician, I began considering whether to bring in other types of interventions and remove Karen from the research study. The waiting period paid off however when the Lord began revealing His truth in the fifth TPM session. In retrospect, it now seems the Lord let Karen get a lot of her pain "off her chest" before providing healing. Karen was thrilled when she began experiencing God's presence in her memories, "This is heavy stuff! You're totally out of yourself and your logic, which is really good. Whenever we go through that truth it's painful at the time, but then by the time the end of the session roles around I'm more peaceful because I know something I didn't know." Karen was understanding the value of trusting God to lead the process; she was not "leaning on her own understanding" (Prov. 3:5-6).

The Prayer Facilitator's Own Healing

My impatience in the above difficulties, however, illustrates another very important truth about the process of TPM. As the facilitator, my level of success is directly related to my own healing and sense of personal peace in administering the process. Through my own issues, I can get in the client's way of receiving healing. I could have started blaming Karen or trying to control the session. That is why Dr. Smith stresses the importance of practitioners receiving their own TPM ministry.[1]

Key Areas of Ministry & Resolution

Karen's lie-based thinking and negative emotions clustered around four main memory group themes:

A. Family of Origin Issues
B. Food Problems
C. Codependency Issues
D. Negative Body Image

Let's examine what the Lord did in each area.

Family of Origin Dynamics

Karen's family environment provided many memories of invalidation and intimidation. As mentioned in my assessment, her relationship with her father was particularly damaging. His anger, abuse, and over control invalidated her legitimate emotional needs and modeled abusive ways to handle anger.

In one prayer session, Karen reported a memory of a time as a child when she was told to pick up sticks in the yard before her father mowed the grass. He demanded she to do this quickly and spoke in a very gruff, aggressive manner. I probed for Karen's thoughts and feelings. "He'd get mad if I didn't do it perfectly. He was loud and demanded respect."

"How were you feeling, Karen?" I asked.

"It made me afraid. [I felt] unloved and not trusted. I felt lost, invisible and lonely."

"Why were you feeling afraid and lonely?"

"I can't disagree. I don't matter. I'm not necessary."

As was Karen's common fashion, she then drifted to another memory. I followed. She remembered when she was six years old her father was getting angry and pounding his fist on the dinner table.

"I was scared to death. I hated it."

"You do sound frightened," I reflected, "What were you thinking in this fear?"

"I'm just a little kid. If I speak up he might hurt my mom…I want dinner to be over so I can get away." Karen continued with the memory: "Things got thrown and I couldn't do anything about it…I can't stop it. I'm too little. I'm [just] too little. I wish I could do something about it."

With her permission I prayed, "Lord Jesus, Karen's feeling powerless in this memory. She believes she's too little. She can't stop it. She's invisible. What do you want her to know in this situation, Lord? Would You reveal Your truth to Karen in whatever way You choose?"

Karen paused. Her look of anguish faded into a calm, peaceful expression. "I am protected by the love of Jesus Christ. I feel more peace. He loves me…I'm safe and whole." The Lord continued by giving Karen more understanding. "I don't have to be the way my parents were to make a relationship work. I'm free to be me. I don't have to have the control [like my dad]."

Karen's memories of her mother were painful as well. As these surfaced in prayer, Karen realized the following. "I was lonely and I needed my mom….My mother wasn't there for me… She focused on everything but the kids…I'm a burden. I'm not important or necessary. She doesn't want to claim me as hers."

"Karen," I asked, "how does it make you feel that you believe 'I'm a burden' and 'she doesn't want to claim me as her own'?"

"It feels pretty rotten!" she exclaimed. Now she got more and more in touch with her anger at her mother. "I got cheated. I just can't believe it! How can she not see me as special or unique in my own way?!"

We prayed for God's truth. Sometimes the Lord will answer even with anger present (at other times, He wants the person to release the anger to Him first.). Karen experienced spontaneous understanding and empathy for her mother. "She was so messed up herself that she wanted her kids to bring her attention."

The Lord continued to minister to Karen. "I do matter…He's telling me He found me, shaped me and protected me. I can rest in Him. He's been there for me. I feel peace. It's hard to think my mother felt that way, but it helps to understand. I do matter. I see Him taking the pressure [off] to look good and be perfect. I don't have to hold the pressure. I'm right in His sight. Whenever I breathe He's with me."

As Karen continued to work on memories related to her father's angry outbursts and her mother's unavailability, she started reporting improvements in her temper and her marriage. "I feel God's presence more closely," she observed, "I admitted my fear of letting God have control in my marriage. I gave Him everything. All my control, especially of Tom, is given to God. Regarding her temper outbursts, she noted, "I'm definitely feeling my feelings more. I'm admitting when I would like to pull his hair but I'm choosing not to do that because God is in control and when I control myself I have a good day." Karen's decrease in angry outbursts and improvements in her marriage certainly confirmed to me that continuing the course of treatment with Theophostic was appropriate.

Food Problems

Karen's overeating became a vehicle for the expression of feelings of powerlessness and loneliness. As she put it, "Food was my company; somebody to give me comfort." We took her food concerns to prayer. Memories surfaced of her eating patterns from early years, so we explored these and petitioned the Lord for His truth. "I missed not being able to share my day…It was the only thing I [felt I] could control [in my family], the only thing that felt good." As the Lord ministered to Karen, she observed, "The control hasn't worked anyway. It hasn't made my relationship with my husband harmonious. God has made me weak so He can be my strength. Food was a temporary pleasure." In heartfelt prayers, Karen repented of using food instead of the Lord as her spiritual and emotional strength.

This transformation led to new behaviors. Karen stated in another session, "I feel my feelings and I'm not pushing them away or eating over them." She was happier than she had ever been about letting go of the food as a source of comfort. She also compared TPM to a popular spiritually based weight loss program. "That approach helped with my obsession to some degree. At least I wasn't focusing on diet. I got kind of free, but then the food problem kept coming back." We praised the Lord together over her sense of progress. Karen's exercise activities were also becoming much more balanced.

Codependency Issues

Karen believed lies that manifested out through her life as a "need to be needed." She developed an outgoing personality to cope with underlying fears of abandonment and rejection; however, this was a two-edged sword. She realized, "I feel pressure because too many people need me. I used to get good feelings for making people feel better. I needed them to need me because then I felt better about myself…I want to be in control of myself and others. That's when I feel safe."

When we went into prayer over the matter, all she could describe was a bodily feeling of tightness in her stomach. I asked her to focus on those physical sensations and allow the emotions to intensify. As she did this, the Lord brought her to an incident in which her parents were yelling and screaming at each other. "I was downstairs pretending to be asleep and they were upstairs fighting. Their anger scared me. I got all tense inside and my stomach just ached…Maybe if I'm good and make them happy they'll stay together and stop yelling at each other.'"

"Lord Jesus, what is Your truth for Karen in this regard?" I asked.

Karen paused, "I'm the wrong kind of glue. He's the only kind of glue that works…I have peace. The knots in my stomach aren't so strong…I'm not alone even though I've been alone a lot. I hear [from God] that I matter; that I'm necessary…The Lord said, 'Believe me and be still.'"

Hearing from Jehovah Rapha that she cannot be the glue to hold her parents' marriage together was a powerful truth for Karen and brought significant relief. In fact in the next session, Karen reported physical healing. "My back feels better. I don't have tight knots in my stomach and I feel more calm in my breathing." Likewise, the simple admonition the Lord gave to believe and be still brought her a large measure of peace and a sense of His control over her circumstances. The Lord's simple eloquence is so different from my regular secular approach when the client does not want TPM and I have to use my logic as "The Therapist" to help the client restructure his/her cognitions. Jesus does a much more profound work!

As the Lord continued to minister to Karen's codependency issues, she reported major breakthroughs in her relationship with Tom. "This week I just totally surrendered all my control to God. I gave Him my control of Tom and trying to point him in the right direction. I gave to Him all the ways I can be enmeshed with him. I just asked for forgiveness from a very deep place. I asked God to keep me accountable to give Tom time to grow. I don't want to crush his spirit."

Karen was also gaining greater insight into her own part in the marital discord. "I had been accusing him of controlling me and crushing my spirit and now I've realized my part. I've done the same thing to him. Tom knew I'd changed. I just prayed all of a sudden and confessed my control and that I wanted to pull his hair, but I didn't do it. Last night we were just playful and had fun. It wasn't this miserable life I've had for the past four and one half years, when I just want to run away from it all. I've just felt so much lighter all week…Tom's not my source of value [anymore], God is."

Forgiveness, Sin, & Repentance in Theophostic Prayer

Some critics erroneously believe that TPM doesn't deal with sin. Actually, I believe it deals with it more profoundly! Karen's comments above serve as a good example of what happens as the prayer recipient receives ministry from the Holy Spirit. The peace and calm that are experienced in the memory enable the client to gain a greater awareness of the depth of their sin, as seen in Karen's repentance over her controlling ways with Tom. They are often eager to confess their sinful strategies to the Lord and accept responsibility for their actions. This is good fruit.

Negative Body Image

Karen had developed distinct feelings of inferiority in this area. She drifted to several linked memories on her way to healing.

"My dad used to say, 'You could drive a Mac truck through the gap in your two front teeth.'"

"How did that make you feel, Karen?"

"His teasing made me feel not pretty. I wanted to look pretty like my mom. If you're pretty you get a lot of attention. Everybody complimented my mom because she was so pretty. That's what girls should be. That's how you get noticed. Pretty gives you power and gets you somewhere. I saw my mom use her sexuality to manipulate my dad and get what she wanted."

Karen's memories drifted to comparisons between herself and her sister. She saw her older sister as the "star" in the family—someone who was stronger, more self-confident and more attractive than she was. She felt inferior to her, too.

"Why are you feeling inferior?" I asked.

"I'm ugly. She's more beautiful and perfect…I am round and pudgy and that's how people perceive me. That's my role and I need to stay that way."

"Lord, what would you reveal to Karen in regards to these thoughts?"

After a moment, Karen responded, "He's telling me it's His way, not my way. Feeling guilty [shame] is my old role of being round and pudgy and having a boy's name and short hair."

Karen then drifted to a memory of being six years old and playing with her cousin in a shed. He was playing as Karen walked in. When he saw her, he began laughing and teasing her that she was fat. Karen felt shame, guilt, and embarrassment.

"Lord, what do you want Karen to know about this?" I asked.

Karen was quiet for a moment. "I see the cross. He's telling me, 'Give it to me. Look to me. Here's my cross; put your guilt [and shame] on it. You don't need to create situations you feel guilty [and ashamed] about in order to get attention.'" Karen sensed another message in the cross. "I need to trust and obey Him. I just need to surrender so it can be His way. He's showing me that I'm demanding and I need to trust. It feels like God wants peace in my life."

I sat in awe at what God was doing. As we processed this imagery and its truth Karen expressed significant feelings of relief. "That was huge!" She exclaimed.

Truly, the Lord taught Karen that she has a pleasing appearance to Him. "I've thought I don't deserve a good body. Now I feel comfort from God. I don't have to be afraid [about my body's appearance]. I can breathe on Him...I don't have a shovel face and my chin isn't too pointed. I have a good smile and I'm worth the time and trouble. I feel like I bring light and joy into the room and Satan doesn't like that. He wants me to feel depressed and heavy and that God will never lighten the load. But that's not me. I bring light, joy and brightness to people...My real spirit is really young, even though I'm older. [I sense God saying that] the well isn't that deep. It's sweet and nice. 'Try it because you can drink from me. I'll be there to guide and protect you. I'll refresh you,' He's saying."

How interesting that Jesus would use these last words and images with Karen! They fit so nicely with the children of Israel's experience in the desert.

End of Treatment

Little by little, Karen left the Marah she had used to feel significant, safe, and secure. As we worked together for those 14 months, Jesus gave Karen the experience of his Elim through the sweet water and date palms of his truth. When TPM ended, she had let go of her anger and intimidation tactics. She had relinquished the need to be in control, and she no longer felt the pressure to please others. She reported freedom with regards to depending on food for comfort, and she had a healthy acceptance of her body and appearance. Tom confirmed these changes, too.

As she assessed her outcome, Karen observed, "Now I can see life the way Jesus sees life. I look at those who have hurt me through the eyes of Jesus. I see people for what they are – wounded, deceived and maybe even deliberately evil people. But, I can see them with the eyes of Christ." I celebrated Karen's growth with her. No matter what her psychological testing would show, I knew that she had grown spiritually. I would be curious as to her status on our three-month follow-up session.

Three-month Follow-up Interview

Had Karen remained in Elim since treatment ended? In the three-month follow-up interview, Karen and Tom both reported that the physical abuse had stopped. Karen had also maintained a healthy perspective in regards to food and exercise, and her codependency traits were no more. Below are excerpts from the videotaped three-month follow-up session with Karen, which appear to indicate that yes, indeed, Karen had met Jehovah Rapha in treatment.

With regard to her anger, Karen said, "It's not fair of me to explode on people because things didn't go my way. I can trust now that God will work it out. God revealed to me that I need to give him my anger instead of everybody else. I don't need to switch the blame. I do that when I don't feel good about my body and eating. That one session [with the cross image] was huge for my life. I've lived by mistrust. God said, 'Give me the guilt and anger instead of everybody else.'...God brought me to the shed. When my cousin said to me, 'You look different. You're different than your sister and you're fat'…This person hasn't been in my life for 20-some years. The shed is just some broken down tin can that they put their lawn mower in. I have no reason to remember any of it except God brought me back to that place and He also made me realize that was a real thing in my life…And I realized my cousin is wrong. God sees me as special and people see me as special…And the next thing you know there's the cross. It was the first time I've ever felt the cross was for me. I've seen a million Easter plays. I believe it. I don't doubt that I have salvation. But, it was so personal for me. I saw Jesus on the cross with the nails in His hands. And He said, 'Look up to me. You don't need to feel guilty anymore. Give me the guilt instead of everybody else. You don't need to create situations to feel guilty anymore. The snow is white because you are pure.'"

With regard to her husband, Karen said, "Satan has run my life by guilt [and shame]. If I didn't feel guilty about my eating I'd figure out something else to feel guilty about. Or, I'd switch the blame because I was so totally insecure. I'd attack my husband because I wanted him to affirm me. When he didn't I'd get angry and then I'd feel so guilty and horrible about myself. And then God showed me His cross and I realized God could take this guilt. I gave it to Him and it was gone. I don't know how I could feel so horrible and then feel so absolutely great."

"God proved to me I could trust Him. I used to believe it more for others than for me, but He proved to me that I could trust Him. He can take my guilt and after I gave it to Him on the cross I felt completely guilt-free. In fact my husband and I even laughed about it together three days later. God is showing me, 'Put it into the nails. Just give me the guilt [& shame]. That picture was so powerful. And He showed me where it all came from. It was such a personal way that God spoke to me. God gave me a two-dimensional picture so I could believe the truth. That picture was so vivid and so real and so personal to my situation and me. It's my personal truth and I can cling to it. That picture definitely is a blessing. I've lived that lie for so many years. Now I focus on those nails. 'Give me the guilt. I can take the guilt.' God can take it so why do I need to walk around with it?"

With regard to her family of origin, Karen said, "And then in another session God showed me how I get to places with my body or work and I just stay stuck. God showed me that because I'm my parents' only biological child I had felt it was my responsibility to keep them together and that because they didn't stay together it was my fault. The truth that He showed me was that I couldn't be the glue. I thought I was the glue to keep them together and God said, 'You're the wrong kind of glue. I'm the only kind of glue that works.' I think I've never grieved my parents' divorce until I came here. And I've been able to share that with other people, too. I tell them this is a lot harder than you think it is. What my parents did to me I've dealt with for the first time in 38 years. That's so powerful for me. I'm not just a survivor who is just coping. The world wants us to just deal with our pain and move on. God showed me to be real…[and] you know what? My husband and I aren't the only ones going through this. People just don't like to talk about their problems. They lie. Most people think I'm a pretty nice person and wouldn't believe I have it in me to go so flipping nuts. But, I do. But that makes me more human and real. It makes people feel like maybe they can open up and that God can help them too. My freedom is that I don't need to walk around with this shame that I kicked my husband. I feel bad and I don't diminish that that was wrong and hurtful and brought pain to us, but we're past that. There's freedom and thank God we can laugh about it."

It's amazing because him seeing my walk with Christ and my realness makes him feel safer to look at his own insecurities. He's feeling safer to be himself and realizes it's okay to admit he has a critical spirit. Everybody knows it anyway. Because of what God did for me I really see him being more humble and real."

Direct questions about TPM During the 3 Month Interview

1. *How is TPM different from your other counseling experiences?*
"For me, it's the most trust I've ever put in God. Coming here, not knowing where God was going to take me, having no idea what He was going to bring up in my past was a huge trust step. There can be a lot of fear in that. What if I found out I was raped or incested? Do I really want to know that? I didn't know what was going to come up for me. What I experienced in TPM was very real and very painful. But because I put my complete trust in Christ it created a real personal connection and it put me in a place to listen to God. I learned I could know that what I was learning was truly from God because it was unique to me. It's God. You don't have to question it.

"I think the only thing that can set people free from all their strongholds is Christ. He gives the lasting peace and freedom. I believe that. I've done other counseling and I would just talk about my problems. What worked here is that I didn't leave here and feel like I did all the talking and I didn't even know what you think. This was totally trusting God. God is the teacher. He's the counselor. He's the best counselor. By being centered on God I can't be focused on the external. I just listened for His voice. Who wants to go to a counselor for the rest of their life?"

"The other thing about TPM is that I'm not hooked into you. With all the co-dependency issues I've had it would be very easy to think, 'Oh, Terry. He's my counselor. He's who I'm going to.' TPM is really healthy because it helped me be more dependent on Christ and that's helping me be free from being codependent…It really showed me being stuck on Christ and listening to Him is much healthier."

2. *What about the pain that you had to face?*
"It's very hard at the moment. It's like somebody stabbed you. It's very hard. It freaks you out because you had no idea your cousin just told you something bad. You're in shock and you're sad and you feel it. You embrace it. It's like you're going in this room with this lie and you totally feel it, embrace it, hug it and then detach from it and let God give you the truth. By feeling and confronting the lie it takes away the power of the lie. It takes away the power when you get the truth. Then you have something that is so much brighter and lighter. My motto now is 'To be real is to heal.' [This is] my prayer for myself."

3. *Did TPM help you find the source of your problems?*
"Definitely! I found the lies. I had all these puzzle pieces to my life and every time a lie was uncovered I felt like I just got this huge chunk of my life that was missing and all of a sudden, I had such relief. I knew what it was and it made so much sense to me and why I am the way I am and why I react the way I react."

"People just want this magic to come to them. I would have wanted you to say, 'Karen, this is what this is about. You're just codependent and do you know what? It bothers people when you smother them.' You can tell me that and then I can make you God. 'Oh, everything that Terry says is right!' This way I had to listen to my heart and soul and decide with God what was right. When I did that it was lasting. God's truth is lasting and you just know that."

Truly, Karen knew how to say, "Heal me, O LORD, and I will be healed; save me and I will be saved, for Thou art my praise" (Jeremiah 17:14).

Karen's Testing Results

Karen's personal testimony was quite moving. As noted previously, her story of healing bears some similarities to Joan in our Introduction chapter, except that Karen used exercise and temper outbursts instead of purging. Like Joan, Karen gave up the lies that fed these coping behaviors, leaving her free to live a much more balanced, fulfilling life. Karen however was different from Joan in another way. She had testing done to see if the results supported her sense of immense progress and healing. These findings, along with the Independent Reviewer's evaluation, supported her testimony.

Substantial psychological symptom reduction can be seen in the graphs of the SCL 90R. Remember, decreasing scores reflect improvement:

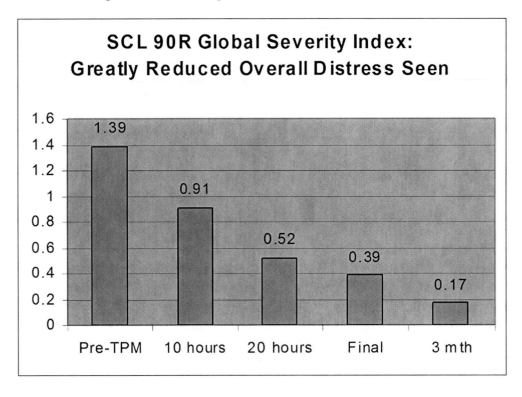

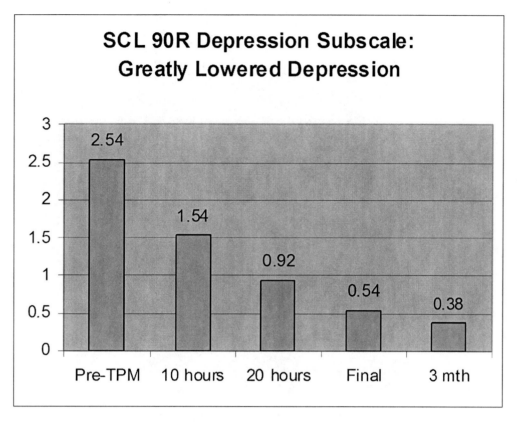

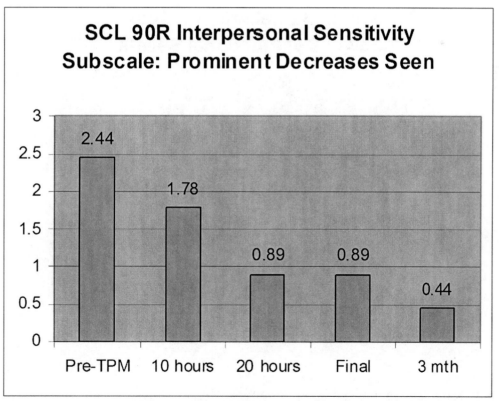

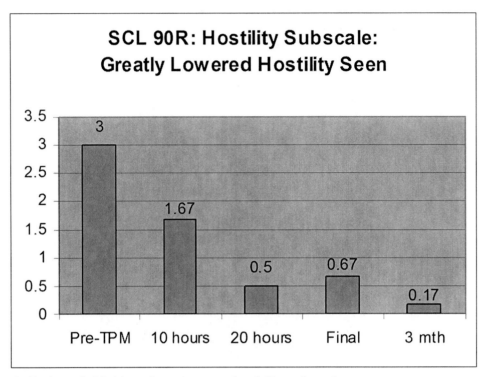

Karen's lie-based thinking also was meaningfully reduced:

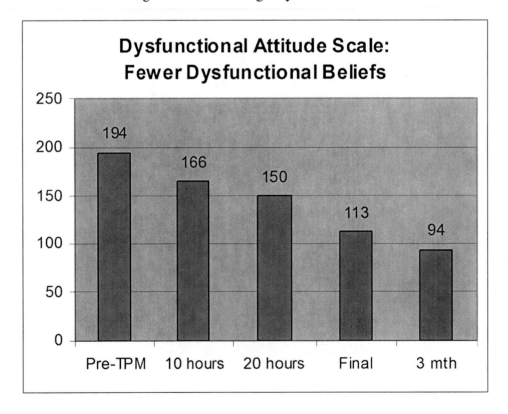

Finally, Karen's spiritual well-being improved. Higher scores indicate increased spiritual well-being:

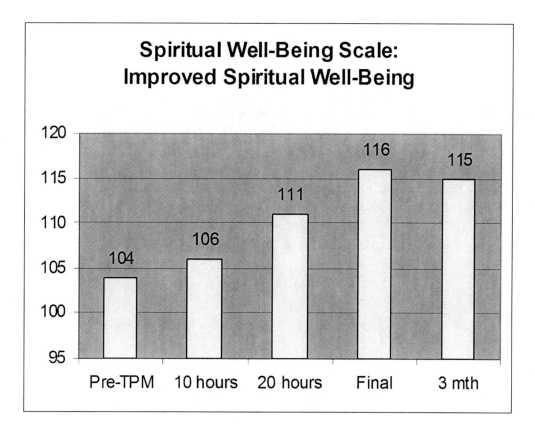

**Spiritual Well-Being Scale:
Improved Spiritual Well-Being**

The Independent Reviewer likewise confirmed Karen's outcome. The reviewer noted "much reduction in symptoms" (the highest rating possible) for each of Karen's diagnoses. In the reviewer's overall evaluation of "How mentally ill is the patient at this time?" Karen was rated as being normal.

Discussion

Karen's case reflects a clearly positive outcome with a client who had tried many different therapies in the past. Because of the spousal abuse taking place, I (Fernando) was glad she was seeing an excellent mental health professional like Terry. He carefully evaluated the pro's and con's of keeping her in this study, and he had some clear ideas about alternative treatment options should those be needed.

Terry also handled quite nicely those early sessions of TPM in which it appeared he might be "stuck." His cultivation of a supportive relationship with Karen helped her feel encouraged enough to continue the process until the Lord began speaking truth. The wait was well worth it, too. Karen experienced the Lord in a deeply intimate way as Jehovah Rapha. Truly, "The Lord who heals" transformed her soul and saved her marriage.

About the Treating Clinician

Terry Zuehlke, Ph.D., has worked in the mental health field since 1974. His experience encompasses the treatment of adults, couples, and adolescent clients as well as work in forensic psychology. He has gained experience at various mental health departments and founded Pathways Psychological Services, P.A. in 1993. Since 1998, he has extensive experience working with diverse populations using a cognitive-behavioral approach with a spiritual focus (Theophostic Prayer) as well as personal and spiritual conflict resolution (The Steps to Freedom in Christ). Together with Dr. Neil Anderson, Terry and his wife, Julie, have co-authored *Christ-centered Therapy: The Integration of Theology and Psychology*. He can be reached at Pathways Psychological Services, P.A. at 763-525-8590, Ext. 304.

Chapter 2 References

1. Smith, Edward (2002). Advanced Training Level One. New Creation Publishing.

Chapter 3

Gloria Meets El Roi: "The God Who Sees Me"

Julie Zuehlke, MSN

In Genesis chapter 16, Hagar was experiencing much mistreatment. She had just given birth to a son (Ishmael) for Abraham. Sarah (Abraham's wife) had initiated this dubious plan as an attempt to answer God's promise of a son for the family. Now Sarah was jealous of Hager and treating her harshly. Hagar fled the abuse, but was feeling desolate and alone. In this place of despair, the Lord personally revealed Himself to her as El Roi, "The God who sees me". The Lord comforted Hagar and gave her insight and promises that enabled her to face the situation. Could He do the same for my client, Gloria?

Julie Zuehlke, MSN.

Gloria sought help for anxiety and trust issues arising from disappointing relationships with men. Now forty-two, she had most recently been in a three-year relationship with a boyfriend, but she ended it several months earlier. Sadly, her relationship issues were not new. She had dated scores of men since her divorce, with similar issues surfacing each time. These transitory relationships had had their impact. Gloria stated, "It's a struggle; I never relax; I'm always on the verge of bailing; I leave the man before he leaves me." She wanted to work on the causes for her repeated break-ups, since her desire to remarry was strong. Indeed, getting dates was not a problem for Gloria. She was an attractive professional woman with a business management degree and modeling experience on the side. Beautiful and disciplined externally, she was lonely and insecure internally.

Gloria's family history revealed clues as to the source and origin of her anxiety and trust issues. Although she knew these clues cognitively, it wasn't enough to heal her wounded emotions. Only the Lord Jesus Christ, speaking truth into the historic events in Gloria's life, could set her free and heal her frequent disconnections in male relationships.

Gloria's Story

Gloria was born to an unwed mother. To make matters worse psychologically, her father was a married man. Her mother kept the pregnancy a secret from the father, and gave her up

39

for adoption when she was seven days old. She was kept in a foster home for three months until an adoption was finalized, and then taken into her new family.

Gloria described her adoptive father as detached and quiet, and her adoptive mother as controlling and hard to please. Her only sibling was an adopted behaviorally disruptive boy, ten years her senior, who had been adopted at age nine after multiple foster home placements. Her father severely physically abused her brother with belt whippings for misbehavior. The brother sexually molested Gloria one time when she was six.

Gloria accepted Jesus as a little girl and attended church regularly. However, the family home was legalistic. This legalism did not communicate love and grace, which is authentic Christianity. Gloria was popular at school, but was forbidden by her parents to accept the honor of being selected homecoming queen because it involved being present at a dance.

To "escape from the home", Gloria married at age seventeen. The marriage produced three children, now adults, and lasted fifteen years. The husband, like her father, was emotionally unavailable, working continually, moving the family over twenty times for work purposes. "I have felt alone all of my life, abandoned again and again," she stated. She stopped worshiping at her legalistic church after the divorce due to the "judgmental attitude others had toward my divorce." Following the divorce, she studied for three years, receiving a business management degree, and was an outwardly successful firm manager and homeowner. However, the internal picture was different. Loneliness, anxiety, and dysfunctional male relationships plagued her.

Assessment

Gloria had experienced some sporadic counseling prior to seeking Theophostic Prayer Ministry. She was troubled by symptoms of anxiety, irritability, mild insomnia, tense muscles, decreased concentration, and obsessive thinking about personal problems described as "constant worry". She had started experiencing panic attacks, and found herself increasingly indecisive, being perfectionist, and filled with interpersonal attachment anxieties.

The following is the professional Individual Treatment Plan, which is required in the clinic in which Gloria was seen. This may be of interest to professionals who utilize Theophostic Prayer in the professional setting. For others, you may want to skip this section.

INDIVIDUAL TREATMENT PLAN

Client Name: Gloria Brown   Date of Birth: 3/30/61

Subscriber Name: Same   Health Plan Name: LXLX

Presenting Problem: After a divorce, showed a pattern of transitory relationships with men. Trust and abandonment issues. Last breakup occurred after a three year unstable relationship experience.

DSM-IV (5 AXIS)

Axis I: Generalized Anxiety (300.02); Spiritual Conflicts (V62.89)
Axis II: Deferred (799.9).
Axis III: Excellent health.
Axis IV: Psychosocial stressors:
            Type(s)   Social environment, Family of Origin   Severity: Moderate
Axis V: Current GAF: 65
            Highest GAF past year: 65

I. PRESENT SYMPTOMS SUPPORTING DIAGNOSIS
Anxious, on edge, irritable, middle insomnia, tense muscles, concentration diminished, obsessional about personal problems, "constant worry", indecisive, perfectionistic, attachment anxieties, recent panic attacks.

II. RELEVANT FAMILY AND SOCIAL HISTORY
Adopted as an infant. No contact with birth parents. Adoptive parents: Mother—controlling, Father—quiet, passive, absent for work. Older adopted brother with behavioral problems. Sexually molested by him one time. Married young, three adult children, divorced after fifteen years, no contact with ex-husband. College degree, self-supporting.

IV. PREVIOUS MENTAL HEALTH SERVICES   Consulted: Y/N   N/A
Minimal, episodic.

V. CURRENT IMPAIRMENTS ATTRIBUTABLE TO DIAGNOSIS
Worry, Obsessions, Relationship Dysfunction

VI. SPIRITUAL HISTORY
Accepted Christ as a little girl, legalistic Christian church, regular attendance until divorce. Now attending an evangelical church. Consistent Bible study.

TREATMENT PROCEDURES	
GOALS RELATIVE TO IMPAIRMENTS	**OBJECTIVE CRITERIA FOR DISCHARGE**
Obsessions 1. Develop healthy cognitive patterns of thinking that lead to decreased obsessional thoughts and anxious feelings.	1. Identify key life conflicts from the past, using cognitive behavioral therapy with Christian imagery to dislodge lies/misperceptions.* 2. Identify major categories of lies believed, replacing them with truth. 3. Complete Freedom Step 2.
Relationship Dysfunction 2. Eliminate pattern of transitory male relationships.	1. Maintain a consistent relationship with a compatible male, ending the relationship due to mate selection criteria, rather than internal fears. 2. Complete Freedom Step 7.
Sexual Abuse Victim 3. Resolve family of origin issues, releasing emotions, and establishing realistic self-perceptions.	1. Identify beliefs formed in childhood resulting from the trauma, resolving them through forgiveness, renouncing of vows, setting of appropriate boundaries. 2. Complete Freedom Step 3.

MODALITIES: Individual

Medications (name, dosage): None

Prescribing Physician: N/A   **Consulted:**   Y/N   N/A

DURATION/FREQUENCY: weekly sessions

Therapist   Julianne S. Zuehlke MS, RN, CS   Date: xxxx
Client   Gloria Doe   Date: xxxx

Course of Treatment

After the initial appointment and history taking, Gloria was given an introductory book to Theophostic Prayer (Healing Life's Hurts... is now available) and a short audiotape, both of which explain the basics of the Theophostic process. At the second session, a verbal explanation of the Theophostic principles was given, at which time she could also ask questions about TPM.

Preparation Time

In my experience, taking the time in the beginning like this to develop a relationship, explain the process, and answer questions greatly enhances the recipient's response. When

TPM principles are applied without appropriate preparation, the client can be "triggered" and may experience wariness, distrust, and hesitancy.

The total Theophostic treatment time was five weekly sessions within two months, and two more sessions spaced out due to work changes and scheduling conflicts, for a total of seven sessions.

Gloria's Theophostic Process

Gloria was motivated and ready to work. Our first TPM session would be productive.

Theophostic Session One: Protective Withdrawal Changed to Trust.

Memory #1: Kindergarten

As we began the prayer time, I asked Gloria to focus on any emotion, physical sensation, or memory event that she may be aware of as a starting place. Gloria closed her eyes and drifted to a recollection of the first day of kindergarten when her father drove her to school in his truck. She remembered carrying her new dolly. They arrived early before others were at the school, and when she asked her dad to wait, he said he wouldn't. He dropped her off and left. She was frightened, fearful, and sad. I empathized with her feelings and then chose one to explore. "Why are you feeling sad?" I asked.

Weeping softly, Gloria responded, "I'm all alone, my feelings don't matter...why did he ever adopt me if he does not care enough to wait?"

I sensed her wound of abandonment. We asked Jesus for his perspective. After a pause, she commented, "I see Jesus with huge arms coming from behind and giving me a big bear hug. He is telling me I am not alone anymore, and that I am so special to him. He planned me from the beginning, and even if I was a mistake to everyone else, He planned for me".

Gloria received this ministry, and the Lord caused an internal awareness within her that she had made a promise (a vow) to herself in that memory event that "I can't cry, I can't show that I am little and vulnerable so I have to be tough." Gloria knew that this vow had affected her all her life. When we asked Jesus what He wanted her to do with that vow, He gave her the sense that she needed to give it over to Him. She prayed to cut off that vow, and announced, "I can show the God given emotions I have and I can rely on God's strength." Her tears ceased, and she had a smile of relief on her face. I quietly thanked the Lord for what He was doing.

Vows

It is not unusual for vows to be found in childhood memories. Vows are commitments or unconscious decisions made to oneself that serve a protective function. A vow is as powerful in the spiritual and emotional world, as a signed legal contract in the physical world. Until the vow is released, it stands as a sentinel keeping truth from being revealed. It can be understood as a willful human effort to accomplish safety that only Jesus Christ can provide. He is our Protector. He will stand "outside" the vow, so to speak, and allow us to willfully solve our problem of vulnerability ourselves, until we choose to renounce the vow, and renew our reliance on him. Examples of vows are: "I'll never cry", I'll never let him know he hurt me", I'll get even someday". Even though the vows were done when an innocent child, it is important to address them. Since the time of this case, Ed Smith has shared some new thoughts on how to deal with vows in his 2007 basic training manual edition. We now realize that all vows are held in place by a lie. The current approach for dealing with vows is to identify the lie holding it in place and receive truth. When this occurs the vow becomes impotent. We encourage you to get his latest basic training manual available.

Memory #2: The Horse

We had plenty of time in the session so I asked, "Lord, is there anywhere else You want Gloria to go today?" She chose to look at a second memory. She was as a three year old in a white coat, cap, leggings, and boots, standing in white snow. "Dad had sold his horse to a new owner, but the horse is resisting entering the horse trailer to be taken away. Dad is beating the horse to force it into the trailer". She felt fear and terror. A flurry of thoughts emerged. "Dad loved the horse. How could he be so mad at something he loved? He doesn't need the horse anymore. He doesn't need me. He'll send me away, too. If I'm really good, I won't get sent away like the horse. Mom said to my brother that if he was not good, they would send him away. They beat him just like the horse."

As Gloria continued experiencing the memory, the most intense core belief surfaced: "I can't be sure of anyone. I can't trust." We asked for the Lord's perspective on this. Gloria waited on His presence. Quietly, she responded, "Jesus is beside me...I see him with me in lots of places in the house, and he is sitting beside me on the steps when my brother was being beaten...Jesus is telling me, 'I am your daddy, and you can come close to me where it is safe!'"

Memory #3: Infancy

Gloria then moved to a third memory. I simply "followed" her. This one contained a sense of being an infant, and her controlling mother not allowing anyone else to hold her. She was in touch with fear, and the core belief that "It is not safe to be held by anyone else."

Womb and Infant Memories

Sometimes recipients of Theophostic Prayer report infant or even womb memories. These experiences are never suggested to clients; rather, clients come to the conclusion that they are in this state themselves. Are these literal memories or merely symbolic images? We're not sure. Certainly God has the ability to do either. If the "memory" has feelings associated with it and resulting core beliefs, we just treat it like other experiences in TPM. There is research emerging about early development that is most interesting regarding developing infants' ability to recognize their mother's voice and other stimuli. We can't be dogmatic about this in either direction, but do acknowledge that we don't know all there is to know about our complexity as special creations of the Lord. This is discussed more in the 2007 edition of the TPM Basic Training materials.

Memory #4: Generational Abandonment

Gloria also became aware that her adoptive dad experienced abandonment through the death of his mother, and her adoptive mother likewise experienced an abandonment by her mother. She had known these facts previously but now these parts of family history took on new meaning for her: She was not the only one who had experienced abandonment in her adoptive family. She believed that the Lord led her to renounce any generational influences of abandonment in her family. As she did this, she experienced a strong sense of Christ's presence, and his promise that she will never be alone because He loves her and has a plan for her life. This practice is not something that is taught in TPM or encouraged but since this was what she wanted to do I did not discourage her.

I (Julie) wish we would have had more time to fully process all that God did in this first session. When we briefly processed her first experience, she stated, "A key belief I had growing up was that my feelings didn't matter. At home I felt lonely and often engaged in protective withdrawal. Now I feel different--so comfortable and at peace, so contented."

Theophostic Session Two: Invalidation Changed to Trust

Gloria's second session proceeded in a similar fashion to her first one. We started by reviewing her experience of the first session, which she continued to feel was very productive, and then proceeded to pray.

Memory #1: The Outhouse

Gloria evidenced the presence of core beliefs of powerlessness, invalidation, and lack of trust all contained in one significant memory. Gloria entered a memory of visiting a relative on a farm with her mom when she was six and her brother was sixteen. "My brother is approaching me from behind the barn, asking me to come and see some raccoons. He is taking me to the outhouse and insists that I come in to see the raccoons inside. I feel strange. He's locking the door. He's having me go to the bathroom, and he is standing and watching me. He touches me and wants me to touch him. He is taking my hand to make me touch him—I just stand there and don't do anything. He makes me promise to not tell mom. I don't know what to do. I am so scared and confused."

Memory #2: The Kitchen

Gloria's memory then moved to her mother fixing dinner in the kitchen at home afterwards. I bit my lip and followed her (I really wanted to stay with the Outhouse memory) but I followed TPM protocol and did not try to influence the direction she was choosing to go. "I am telling her [mom] what my brother had done. She tells me not to tell anyone, and says it was okay that it was me and not someone outside of the family. I feel so bad." Then, the core belief in this memory surfaced.

Gloria sobbed, "I don't matter. There is nobody to protect me. I'm expendable." Tears streamed down her face as she embraced these lies. I asked the Lord to reveal His perspective to her. Gloria paused and listened, "He is telling me it is not okay it was me. That is never okay.

45

I'm as white as snow in front of Jesus. I am innocent. I have a precious little heart." She then had a strong sense from the Lord that she needed to forgive her mom. When I asked her if she was willing to do so, she affirmed her willingness. She then lifted multiple offenses from her mom up to the Lord, such as her mom's lack of protection, self-centeredness, and the lack of genuine spiritual influence in the home.

Memory #3: Back to the Outhouse

After this experience she found herself back in the former memory. "My brother is touching me, and it hurts, ouch". Gloria says, "I'm so scared, I'm frozen, and I'm shut down. I can't feel, I can't comprehend, and I'm overwhelmed". In the midst of her pain, I asked the Lord to reveal to Gloria what he wanted her to know about these beliefs. Gloria reported, "Jesus is lifting me up and out of the outhouse! My brother is all alone in there—I'm gone! Jesus is stroking my long braids. He is wiping my tears, and is telling me how much He loves me. He says I am special, and that I can trust Him". When I asked her how true that felt, she gave a resounding, "Oh, that feels very true!"

The Lord is in Charge

This session illustrates how the Lord is in charge and I do not need to guide or direct where the individual goes in his/her memories. Instead of revealing his truth regarding the sexual abuse when the outhouse memory first came into focus, instead she dealt with her mother's offenses of lack of affirmation and protection, and the need to forgive her. Gloria then moved back to the outhouse scene where the Lord revealed the truth to her. When the first outhouse memory changed to the kitchen scene, my thoughts were, "Lord, don't leave the outhouse! She needs healing there!" If the facilitator "leans on his/her understanding" and attempts to direct the session, he/she most likely will be out of sync with what the Lord desires to accomplish. In my experience supervising new learners of Theophostic principles, this one is sometimes difficult to grasp and practice.

Memory #4: Generational Cleansing

During the end of this second prayer session, two memories came to the surface, one as an adult in which she is being told that her brother's wife left him due to his revealed sexual addiction, and another as a child in which she is being told that her birth father was a married man when he fathered her with her birth mother. She believed that the Lord revealed to her mind the need to pray against any generational spirits passing to her from the trauma of the abuse, and to confess the unlawful union of her birth mother and father. She prayed according to this leading. Here again this was not TPM protocol but she desired to do this.

We were at the end of the hour, and, as I typically do, I indicated this in prayer to the Lord, and asked Him to bring whatever closure he wanted for the session. Gloria was silent, listening, and said, "Jesus is telling me that He makes all things new." She said this with joy in her countenance, which was such a contrast from the weeping and the pain at the beginning. Seeing the Lord transform pain into joy is one of the many delights of ministering Theophostic prayer with recipients. I am blessed that recipients allow me to participate as a witness!

Theophostic Session Three: Interchangeability Changed to Trust

As you may have surmised from reading my session one account, when I start prayer in the session, I have the person began to focus on any emotion, physical sensation, or memory event that might surface. [Editor note: A facilitator should never ask the Lord to surface memory, take people to memory, help them to feel emotion, etc. Though this was an early teaching in this ministry approach it has long since been abandoned and is no longer taught or practiced by TPM facilitators. It is believed that people will go where they need to go and feel what they need to feel when they are willing and ready. It is taught in the training that the Lord will not take people anyplace they are not willing to go less He violate their will.] This time, Gloria reported experiencing pain in her epigastria area. I asked her to focus on that sensation since it could have relevance. I asked her to just let it build and to experience all of its sensations, and then asked her if she was willing to allow her mind to connect her with any historic place where she may have felt this sensation before.

Memory #1: Sunday School

Gloria's mom was the children's church Sunday School superintendent for years, and the children loved her. "I often felt insignificant since she gave more attention to them than to me," Gloria quietly noted. The memory scene began after a Sunday School time when eight-year-old Gloria had seen many of the children hugging her mom. "I am asking my mom at home, 'Do you love the other children more than me?' She is pausing, and says, 'I love you all the same.'" Gloria begins to weep softly, revealing deep sadness, and stating her beliefs in this memory, "I'm not special. I'm different. The other kids have moms who love them special. I'm interchangeable. I can't trust another's love for me."

I sensed the depth of this injury to Gloria's sense of worth. "Lord, what is Your perspective on these beliefs? Gloria feels interchangeable. Would You reveal to her Your thoughts on this in the way that You choose?"

Gloria states, "Jesus hurt for me. He is saying that the world makes relationships disposable. I'm special to Him. There is no one else like me. I see a three-stranded cord. Jesus is a part of relationships and knits them together."

Memory #2: Fantasizing About Birth Mom

Gloria continued, "I'm going away from my mom in the memory, and I am fantasizing about my birth mother. If I could be with my birth mom, I'd be loved. Here I am not special. I don't belong. I am misplaced."

I asked the Lord to reveal his perspective to Gloria. She states, "He is telling me that I was a gift, and they did not know how to receive it. I don't have to work at being loved. It's good enough to just be who He made me to be. I need to forgive my parents."

Gloria then offered a prayer of forgiveness for the offenses against her by her parents. She acknowledged that they had hurt her by the absence of good things in her life, and that their neglect was wrong. She acknowledged that she had held on to her anger and hurt because when she was a child, she didn't understand how to release it. She asked the Lord to deal with them

Himself because it was too big for her. She said she forgave them because she knew how hurt they were themselves in their own lives.

Forgiveness

As is often the case in Theophostic prayer, a recipient will have an open heart to forgive offenders after the Lord's truth in the memory event is revealed. This embodies John 8:32: "Then you will know the truth, and the truth will set you free." The forgiveness is not just cognitive or merely "lip service", but comes from a heart that now sees the memory and offender for what they are— events in life over which the Lord has mastery. The recipient can be free of bitterness, revenge, or resentment—free enough to release the offender and offense to the Lord. This is beautiful to witness.

Theophostic Session Four: Disconnection Changed to Trust

Memory #1: Potatoes in Your Ears

Upon my typical opening prayer, Gloria reported a first grade memory in which she asked the teacher to repeat what she had said, and the teacher retorted, "Do you have potatoes growing in your ears?"

Gloria notes, "I am not speaking…my thoughts are in turmoil. I feel so helpless. I want to disappear. I'm different. I'm the only one who didn't hear. I'm defective."

Memory #2: Mother Screaming

While beginning to explore the above memory, Gloria drifted to a second memory so I followed. "My mother is screaming at my older brother. I am very little. I feel so afraid and so helpless. I can't do anything. My dad is leaving the room and doing nothing. I am just pretending that I'm not hearing [her]."

When I asked the Lord for his perspective, Gloria stated, "Jesus is saying my dad was afraid of her. He's saying there's nothing I could have done. It was evil." Gloria continued to be in the memory, because she stated there still was additional pain in it. She identified feeling fear in the memory.

I asked, "Are you willing to focus on that fear?" She said that she was. After a moment, I asked her, "What is your mind telling you about the fear?"

She stated, "People who love you have emotions that can turn on a dime. I need to be cautious. I have to be strong."

"Lord, what is Your perspective?" I prayed aloud.

Gloria stated, "The Lord says I need to renounce the promise I made to myself to be strong on my own. I need to claim the strength of the Lord and His armor." Gloria proceeded to offer this up in prayer, confessing and renouncing the vow, and announcing she will rely on the Lord's strength. I again asked the Lord what else he wanted to reveal to Gloria. She stated, "He says my family was like a sick plant. Love is true, and from God. He wants me to accept love for what it is, and not to protect myself from love." Gloria then stated, "But I still believe that love is dangerous because you may lose it."

"I asked, "Are you willing to go to the place where you learned this thinking and seek to understand the source and origin of that core belief that love is dangerous because you may lose it?" She said she was.

Memory #2: Infancy Foster Home

Gloria's reported an awareness of the three-month period she was in a foster home following her birth. "I love it here. People are wonderful. People are happy." She then states her adult understanding, "I'll never see them again." I sensed the immense sadness in her at this point.

When we asked for the Lord's perspective, she stated, "The Lord is telling me that He gave me the capacity to love. I had it as that infant. My heart was wide open. I can do it again. I renounce the vow to shut down so I will survive if love is lost. I announce that I am free to love. Jesus will help me survive anything. I've been through the worst." Gloria's sadness had now changed to joy at Christ's revelation.

Theophostic Session Five: Dependence Changed to Wholeness

Update

Since the last session Gloria had visited her mother, currently in a nursing home, and indicated it was a positive encounter. She also reported that two friends had given her feedback that her demeanor had changed from a stern countenance to one of increased relaxation and ease. Gloria was excited about both developments. She also reported that she didn't need to work at these two successes. They just "occurred" effortlessly.

Theophostic Prayer Contrasted with Cognitive Approaches

This illustrates a difference between traditional cognitive counseling approaches and Theophostic Prayer. In cognitive approaches the client has assignments to apply positive self-talk in situations in which negative emotions begin to emerge; to pin positive affirmations on the refrigerator and medicine cabinet to recite often during the day; to journal the "A-B-C-D's" for difficult situations. This is human effort. Fine though it is and supported by research, those with weak willpower often fail at this, and persons have to be continually alert to the task at hand in order to feel calm. Theophostic change is Christ-focused empowerment. The negative emotions are reduced because through prayer the core beliefs driving them have been replaced with the Lord's truths. Since research is at such an early stage with Theophostic Prayer, we can't really compare the approaches yet, but we praise God for both.

Memory #1: Camp

As we opened in prayer, the session began with an age thirteen camp memory of a trip to the nurse's office for homesickness. Besides feeling homesick, Gloria was feeling alone and inadequate. Many beliefs emerged as she experienced this memory. "I don't fit in, I'm different, I'm growing too fast, too soon." She also felt uncomfortable and fearful, with core beliefs of "becoming a woman is uncertain for me, I don't want to grow up. I have to leave home if I grow up, and I won't know what to do. Mom controls everything, and doesn't let me handle life experiences. I can't do things for myself. I can't function on my own."

Memory #2: The Tractor

I asked the Lord to reveal His truth or give Gloria the grace and courage to go anywhere else He wanted her to go. She reported remembering a memory at age four, in which she was riding with her mother on a tractor. She was aware of intense fear. "I'm riding with her, standing right next to her. She shows me exactly how to stand. If I don't hold on tight, I'll get run-over. If I do it wrong, I'll die. If I disobey my mom, a horrible thing will happen to me."

I asked Jesus for his perception of this situation. Gloria stated, "Jesus is saying He was taking care of me. It wasn't my mother, it was him."

Gloria then became aware of a sense of suffocation. "Focus on that sense," I told her.

She stated, "I can't get away. Mom is smothering me. I have no separate identity". I sensed Gloria's anxiety and asked Jesus for his perception of this situation.

Gloria pauses, "Jesus is saying that my mom was afraid to lose me. It was not just me hanging on. She was hanging on to me, too."

Memory #3: The Boss

Gloria reported an adult memory of a former boss. "He is sexually harassing me [at work]. I am dodging him and appeasing him." When we asked the Lord to reveal his perspective, she shares, "Jesus is saying I am so complete in Him I don't need someone else to complete me. I am a work in progress. He has promised he will complete me."

This boss memory was significant in that Gloria had a false sense of her identity as a child of God. She was operating out of childhood lie-based core beliefs of fear of dying, fear of being alone, and fear of disapproval, which were fueling her obsessive thinking and adult anxieties. Receiving the truth from the Lord that she is complete in Him gave her the peace and calm which had so long been absent.

Processing Session

Several weeks occurred since the last Theophostic session due to a job change, with inflexible hours preventing appointments given our two schedules. Gloria reported a renewal of her relationship with her boyfriend of three years, and deep emotional intimacy between them. She was open to his pending proposal of marriage. Instead of doing Theophostic prayer this session, we processed her situation. We discussed the importance of a marriage preparation class for the two of them, especially since this involved a second marriage for both. We also discussed the need for her boyfriend to do personal work on the wounds behind his past alcoholism.

Theophostic Session Six: Aloneness Changed to Trust

Update

A few more weeks had occurred before this sixth Theophostic session. Gloria's new job had ended due to an office merger, and she returned to her former position. While in her new job, her boss had made inappropriate gestures, and she responded with an appropriate assertive stance toward his behavior. This showed great progress especially when compared to her previous behavior with her boss's flirtatious overtures. Again, it was "effortless" and almost automatic.

In a dramatic shift, Gloria's boyfriend had ended the relationship due to a misunderstanding he had had with her after a disagreement between them. Prior to treatment, this would have crushed Gloria. Now, she redirected her boyfriend "to search out his own solutions to this and other dilemmas in his life, rather than me rescuing him." Gloria was very pleased with her new behavior, but still feeling some emotional pain.

Memory #1: The Breakup

We went to prayer for the Lord's perspective on this development. She surfaced the recent memory of her boyfriend ending the relationship. She reported feeling "alone, misunderstood, powerless, and shocked". Her core beliefs were that she "was alone, and would always be alone."

I asked the Lord to reveal his perception of this event. Gloria stated, "Jesus is telling me that the day He died was a Friday, and everyone thought it was final, but on Sunday he rose again. No matter how dark a Friday looks, we are third day people. He can bring joy out of sorrow. I am not alone. He is with me. He is holding me by my hand and leading me. He says, 'don't give up hope'. I have great power on my knees because He is all-powerful. Sorrow lasts for a night, but joy comes in the morning."

Post Session Contacts

In several telephone conversations following this appointment, I helped Gloria process different contacts and decision points with her boyfriend. She was handling the ambiguity of her relationship with the boyfriend with a forthright and calm approach, despite the ups and downs. Part of the ambiguity was the entrance of his ex-wife into the picture, and pressure from both sides of their families for them to re-unite.

Theophostic Session Seven: Grief Changed to Trust and Peace

Update

At the beginning of this seventh Theophostic session, Gloria's job had changed yet again; her boyfriend had decided to reconcile with his ex-wife. Sadly, he had also returned to alcohol abuse. Even with all these obvious stressors, Gloria seemed much more centered than in our early sessions.

Memory #1: Back to the Kitchen

When we opened our prayer time, the feelings that first surfaced were anger, confusion, anxiety, and disappointment. I asked Gloria's if she was willing to go to the place where she first had any awareness of these feelings. The memory she entered into was the one we had visited before in the kitchen, after her brother's sexual abuse, where she told her mother that her brother had inappropriately touched her sexually. I asked her why she felt the way she did, she stated, "I can't count on mom. She tells me she loves me, and then she behaves differently. I'm unsafe."

I asked Jesus to give his perspective. She shared, "Jesus is saying that I am worth being protected."

Memory #2: Back to the Breakup

Gloria then entered the recent memory of her boyfriend ending their relationship. She was filled with grief and sadness. "Lord, what do You want Gloria to do with the grief?" I asked.

"Jesus is comforting me. He knows how my heart broke. He gave my boyfriend chances, but my boyfriend wouldn't hear." Gloria then prayed, "I give you, Jesus, my grief. Take it upon yourself."

I encouraged Gloria to stay in the Lord's presence. "Keep listening to what Jesus wants you to know," I said.

She reported, "Jesus wants me to sit on His lap, and let Him put his arms around me. I am doing it. He is replacing my grief with peace. Jesus is taking my broken heart and putting it back in my chest –it is all together!" she exclaimed. She then proceeded, "I need to forgive my boyfriend, since Jesus has forgiven me for a lot."

Gloria prayed to forgive him. "Jesus is saying, 'Stay close to me. We will experience joy together, just as we experienced grief together. I have blessings for you from my hand because you trusted me."

I marveled silently at how far Gloria had come. She had come full circle from not trusting others, to placing all of her trust in Jesus Christ, who was enabling her to weather the ending of this relationship, something she could not have done nearly as well prior to TPM.

As we ended our prayer time, Gloria decided to take some behavioral steps of closure with her boyfriend. She planned to remove memorabilia from him by putting it in a box and placing it in storage. She prepared to see him from time to time, since he was in her circle of friends. She had a calm feeling about this contact. She planned to pursue a relationship with another man whom she had previously dated, and who had expressed a desire to reconnect. It has been three months since this session, and I have received no further updates from Gloria other than the testing.

Theophostic Prayer and Sanctification

In my experience, recipients who have experienced healing truth from Jesus often demonstrate this pattern. The healing is often rapid and freeing, and then "check-ups" occur as the trials of life expose other lies that are believed. We are all in the process of sanctification, that is, becoming more and more like Christ, who is sinless and free of the enemy's deception (lie-free). The Lord has many ways to accomplish sanctification in our lives (prayer, Bible study, fasting, worship, the spiritual disciplines, etc.). Theophostic can also be one of them. In trials, TPM can facilitate a continual process of identifying the "bad feelings" that arise, and then going with Jesus to the source and origin. The increased truth in our lives facilitates repentance from sinful attitudinal and behavioral patterns. One could see this in Gloria's acts of forgiveness. The sanctification process will end when we go home to be with the Lord in eternity, when we will see Him face to face and will have shed our corruptible flesh for the incorruptible, our lie-based core beliefs for His complete Truth, and our sinful actions/attitudes for His manifest holiness.

Testing Results

Julie sensed Gloria had improved and this was reflected in her therapist ratings. Gloria's testing results also confirmed the results. She had a clear decrease in psychological distress, fewer dysfunctional beliefs, and an increased sense of connection with God. The graphs below describe her results. Lower scores reflect improvement on the SCL 90R and DAS, while higher scores indicate improvement on the SWBS.

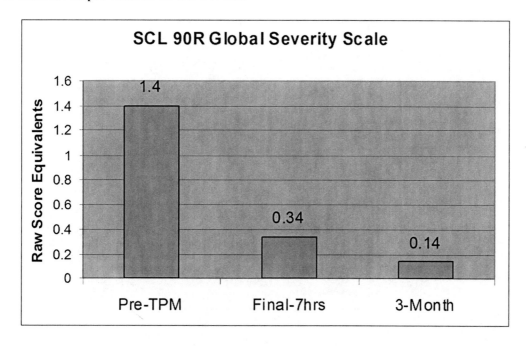

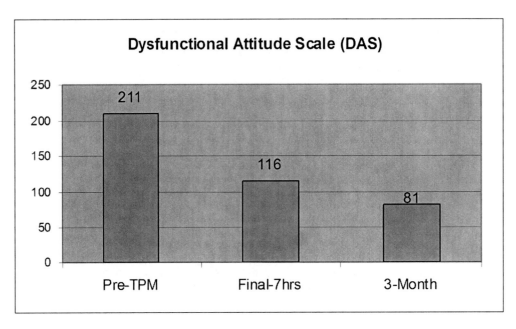

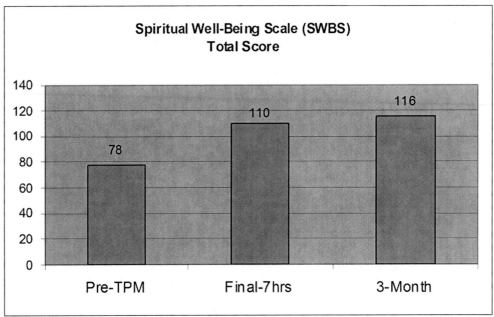

Independent Reviewer's Assessment

A Christian licensed psychologist who does not utilize Theophostic Prayer conducted a review of Gloria's mental health status and progress at the conclusion of Gloria's sessions. This psychologist did not know the type of treatment Gloria had received. Based on her interview with Gloria, as well as an examination of the clinical record, the psychologist rated the current symptom levels as "much improved" (the highest rating possible in every category). She also indicated that Gloria showed no signs of mental illness.

Discussion

As Gloria's sessions revealed, she had major trust issues in relationships that stemmed from her many childhood experiences. She protectively withdrew, felt invalidated, interchangeable, expendable, and disconnected. She initiated ending relationships prematurely, rather than staying until the natural ending, whatever that might be. In the sequence of events with her boyfriend during therapy, she stayed until the natural ending. She was able to experience the feelings of grief and loss, which were realistic and truth based, and engaged in forgiveness and closure. In the past, she likely would have acted on lie-based emotions that emerged from events in her past, and would have ended the relationship prematurely.

Gloria's testing results suggested she had a positive experience. These results were maintained after 3 months. Psychologists reading Gloria's story might react negatively to a couple of parts of her story. First was the sense she had of experiencing some infant and womb memories. They might base this on their evaluation of the current scientific possibility of such occurrences. We (the research team) cannot say conclusively whether the Lord was giving a picture of what occurred or a symbolic image. However, isn't this His choice? He is God and He certainly has the power to do either. Perhaps one's worldview perception of what God can do, will do, and wants to do to heal us influences whether you reject these experiences altogether or whether you see them as something God can possibly use, symbolically or literally. Gloria felt they were from God and very helpful. The other aspect involves Gloria's sense that she had to break some generational transmissions in therapy (for example, a generational transmission of abandonment). Some denominations might react like the psychologists. Therapists who use genograms (diagrams of a family tree, along with information about each family member) however readily see generational transmissions in many instances. They conceptualize such patterns as being influenced by basic learning and modeling in the home environment as well as by genetic influences rather than being from spiritual influences. Certainly, we believe in those influences and would not negate them in any way. We would merely add a consideration of the spiritual as a part of the transmission process as well. It is interesting that Gloria brought up the need for this prayer on her own each time, and that she had a sense that the prayers were very helpful. This is another area in which we often follow the client's lead.

Indeed, clear memory pictures characterized Gloria's Theophostic sessions, along with ease in the identification of lies, and dramatic episodes of Jesus ministering His truth to her both visually and verbally. As the facilitator, I (Julie) felt I was on "holy ground" as I witnessed the Lord so intimately relating to her internal pain. As she would describe the tenderness and compassion of the Lord's illuminations to her mind, I would experience literal "goose bumps" as I was a party in seeing His power in dispelling lies with which the enemy had created strongholds and bondage.

Truly, Gloria experienced the Lord as "El Roi". She no longer felt desolate and alone. God had seen her, and she had seen Him. In her own words, she notes, "I believe, through Theophostic Prayer, I got to the root issues of my problems, and I felt God's power in the healing of my wounds and pain from the past. Other counseling would offer temporary relief but nothing deep and lasting. I am better able to identify when I need Theophostic Prayer Ministry in a problem area than before, and I now know how to bring it to God for healing and to trust the process." Her independent reviewer noted that Gloria stated, "I have grown leaps and bounds. I can help others because I am less self-absorbed. Other close friends have noticed the changes in me." Like Hagar before, Gloria was no longer adrift in the desert of "soon to be loveless" relationships, but was now basking in the sun of the Lord's love. She could trust Him always, even when human relationships might fail.

Footnotes

*We now recommend that the clinician go ahead and name Theophostic Prayer Ministry on insurance forms and then describe TPM in psychological terms that the insurance company can understand, talking with them as necessary about the approach. If the company will not pay for TPM, then fee-for-service arrangements can be made.

**Since the time of this case, Smith has updated his introductory materials with his book, *Healing Life's Deepest Hurts*, which he now recommends as an introduction. The book is available through Theophostic Ministry, Campbellsville, KY, at www.theophostic.com, or call 270-465-377.

About the Treating Clinician

Julianne S. Zuehlke. MS, RN, CS, is a Registered Nurse (RN) with a Master's Degree in Psychiatric-Mental Health Nursing (MS). The American Nurses Association certifies her for Advanced Practice as a Certified Nurse Specialist (CS). Together with Dr. Neil Anderson, Julie and her husband, Terry, have co-authored *Christ-centered Therapy: The Integration of Theology and Psychology*. Julie holds a Ministry License with the Evangelical Free Church of America. She is in full-time vocational ministry on the Senior Staff of Crystal Evangelical Free Church, New Hope, Minnesota, directing Care Ministries, where she has developed a church-based Theophostic Prayer Ministry using lay ministers. She maintains a small part-time caseload in her husband's outpatient Christian mental health clinic, Pathways Psychological Services, Golden Valley, Minnesota, where she applies Theophostic prayer principles with her mental health clientele. She can be reached at Crystal Evangelical Free Church at 763-533-2449 or at Pathways Psychological Services at 763-525-8590.

Chapter 4

Returning Home Safely: Teresa's Journey

Myrna Thatcher, LMFT, Annette Smith, & Fernando Garzon, Psy.D.

God brings our clients to us and, ultimately, He is responsible for their healing. We are simply the human touch that He has placed in their lives as His vessels. We praise God for allowing us to be instruments in the Master's Hand as He divinely reaches down to heal the broken hearted and set the captives free. May our story of Teresa bless you.

Myrna Thatcher, LMFT, & Annette Smith, Lay Counselor

"At times I do not want my husband touching me. I feel so tainted and defective." Teresa, an attractive 27-year-old woman, tearfully told us of her love for her husband John and yet her anxiety at his advances. During their five years of marriage, she had experienced great difficulties in sexual intimacy. After our initial interview with Teresa, we understood why.

Teresa's father sexually abused her for over 17 years. In fact, only in the last two years had she established clear boundaries and a safe life without the abuse. Even in the early years of her marriage, the abuse was continuing. As she was slowly starting to deal with the painful reality of this mistreatment, a sudden ambivalence had emerged towards John. Husbands often become the target of "emotional leakage" in instances like these. Essentially, Teresa felt too ashamed and tainted to relate to her husband. Depression and anxiety became her unwanted companions, challenging her as a stay-at-home mom for her preschool and infant sons.

While Teresa's intake progressed, she poured out a myriad of feelings—shame, anxiety, confusion, powerlessness, anger, and hopelessness. She also noted periods of numbness when the feelings just got to be too much. The more we heard her story, the more we realized just how courageous Teresa really was.

Teresa's Story

Teresa characterized her parents' involvement with her during her childhood as virtually nonexistent. She was raised in a farming community with four other siblings (3 boys and one girl), and she was the second youngest of the family and the youngest daughter. Indeed, Teresa felt like a "wall-flower" growing up. Her mom and dad never attended any of her activities or supported her in her interests. God's grace, however, was present for Teresa in that her parents did drop off the kids on Sunday mornings for church even though they themselves were not Christians. Teresa became a Born-Again Christian during this time.

When Teresa became seven, her dad began using her for his own purposes—sexually. The abuse eventually included full sexual contact within two years and would occur when Teresa's mom was away in town doing activities, or when dad managed to take Teresa to an isolated area of the farmland.

Soon, Teresa felt that all she had to attract a man was her body. Not surprisingly, as a teenager she rapidly sexualized her need for attention from boys, resulting in a sexually promiscuous lifestyle. "No one cared about me so why should I care about myself?" she stated. The love and belonging she sought from her family were only momentarily filled by these relationships and she again felt used and betrayed soon after a breakup.

With three years between them, Teresa and her sister (Susan) had little conflict as children. They shared the same bedroom but had minimal common interests. They did, however, have one thing in common. Both were being sexually abused.

Even as an adult, Teresa felt treated the same as when she was a child—neglected and abused. Her only adult contact with her parents was at family events such as birthday celebrations. Mom seemed distant and really "focused on her own life." And, of course, dad was still playing out the role of the perpetrator. Though Teresa was married with two children, the abuse continued.

A dramatic change took place when Susan started going to therapy. As she started dealing with her own abuse history, she confronted Teresa about hers. This encouraged Teresa to start going to therapy along with Susan and to break the silence. With the therapist, they both informed mom about the abuse. Later, dad was confronted, with Teresa's husband and her mom both present at that confrontation.

It was almost easier for Teresa emotionally before the abuse came out. She knew better how to live with the secret. So did her family. Like many incest families, she was initially blamed for the abuse rather than seen as the innocent victim that she was. Feeding her sense of blame was the fact that everyone was pushing her to "get over it". The secular psychotherapy had been helpful in getting the abuse out, but now treatment quickly focused on Teresa's marriage, leaving her with a wake of feelings about her past. Teresa realized the energy she was expending to "keep it all together" was just too much. She wanted to deal with the issues of her heart.

Susan left the psychotherapy first, feeling it had done some beneficial things but now her progress was also at a standstill. She started working with us for a month and began telling Teresa about the benefit she was receiving from Theophostic Prayer Ministry. Soon, Teresa followed in her sister's footsteps. Thankfully during this time, the family also finally started dealing with dad, and he soon started his own psychotherapy with another therapist voluntarily.

Assessment

Teresa described depression, anxiety, and sexual intimacy difficulties, all common consequences of her traumatic life. She feared her biological family would abandon her and she was in touch with many powerful feelings, though numbness sometimes occurred when these were too overwhelming. Interestingly however, she only felt her anger mildly. After having been abused for over 17 years, one should be a little angrier than that! Therefore, this would be one feeling that Teresa would need to realistically confront.

Course of Treatment

At the initial appointment, Teresa was given an introductory book on Theophostic Prayer which explained the Theophostic process. It was important for her to be fully aware of what to expect from the ministry times. After our intake session, subsequent sessions focused on the Theophostic process and developing homework assignments to augment the work. For example, a person must feel their feelings at a heart level for God to heal them. Since Teresa in her daily life became numb when the feelings got to be too much, we realized journaling would be a helpful tool to keep her experiences from becoming too overwhelming. Journaling strategies are commonly used in treating sexually abused clients. Sessions were usually one hour in length.

Repressed Emotions

Repressed emotions are hidden feelings that lie buried and can take time to surface. Clinical research has established the importance of acknowledging and processing difficult emotions when dealing with traumatic past events.[1] Sometimes these feelings are very new for people receiving ministry. Processing guardian lies around the perceived need to maintain the repression and doing homework assignments like journaling about the event can help bring the feelings to the surface. See the Smith's latest Basic Training Manual (2007 at the time of this writing) for more information on processing guardian lies.

Teresa's Theophostic Process

In the early sessions, Teresa expressed a wide spectrum of feelings. The sometimes contradictory emotions contained in her statements did not surprise us:
"I love him because he is my dad but I hate him as a person."
"I am relieved it's out in the open and that it won't happen again [but] I feel disloyal to dad because I have revealed the abuse."
"I want to feel angry but then I don't want to feel angry."
"I feel disloyal to mom because dad is her husband and I am afraid that she will leave him now."
When exploring these feelings and various historical events in prayer, we often asked Jesus if there are any other feelings that Teresa needed to experience right now in viewing the past. Normally, she sensed the answer immediately—anger. "Dad put me in this position to have to go through all this. He has turned my life upside down! . . . Does he really care that he abused me?! He's more worried about himself than he is about me." Dealing with repressed feelings like anger would be an important part of Teresa's treatment.

In each of these early sessions, we would go slowly, talking with Teresa about her many feelings and the core beliefs underlying them. We would empathize with her and confirm to her how reasonable it was for her to be angry. When it felt like we had processed the anger enough, we asked her if she was willing to give the anger to Jesus. She bravely said yes and meant it. Quietly we prayed together. We acknowledged that it was only the Lord's grace that could lift this anger off of Teresa, and we asked Him to do it. After a few moments, Teresa had a sense of Jesus' loving presence and the anger being lifted off. Her tears and big sigh of relief confirmed to Annette and me that Jesus had started His work. One layer of anger was gone. We knew however that there would be more so we reminded Teresa of this fact. An abuse wound this big has many layers of hurt and anger and it will take some time to process each one.

Homework assignments helped Teresa get more in touch with her feelings. For example, we had Teresa write a story about what her father did to her. We asked her to begin at the earliest age that she could remember, write about the event(s), and to explore the feelings God brought up in each memory she recalled. To help her with this assignment, we gave her a feelings identification sheet to help her recognize how she felt in each event (The feelings sheet is simply a list of feelings to help the person identify how they feel.) [Editor's note: Homework assignments are not a part of the TPM training but was done by this therapist.]

Numbness

Numbing occurs when a person experiences powerful emotions and s/he feels unsafe or unable to process these feelings. The emotions can be from the current situation or surfacing from a past trauma that is similar in some ways to the present event. Teresa becoming numb when her husband made sexual advances at her is a classic example. A big part of this numbness was from the emotions she experienced in her father's abusive advances. We see numbing as a God-given "safety valve" that helps a person function until they're in a safe environment to work through whatever is stirring in their heart.

Teresa would do her homework, which helped greatly in her prayer process. For example, in one session, she brought in some writing on a memory of when she was 8 years old and was hiding in the barn from dad. She didn't want dad to find her because then he would sexually abuse her. She described feeling panicky, hopeless, scared, guilty, and angry. As we started the Theophostic process around this memory, the Lord gave her a revelation in regards to why she used so much repression and dissociation in regards to her feelings. She realized that as a child there was nowhere else to go with these feelings. She just closed herself off to the world because it was not safe to be open and feel her emotions. Repression and dissociation were a God-given survival mechanism for her. Now, the Lord was asking her to let Him be her defense instead.

In another memory, Teresa was in junior high and her dad was abusing her in an isolated field. "I feel so ashamed. He is making me touch him and I don't want to . . . I should be able to stop him but I just don't know how . . . Why is he doing this? Why me?" As we continued prayerfully processing the memory over a couple of sessions, a key emotional defense she experienced was numbness. Therefore, we focused on identifying the beliefs associated with that occurrence. "I can't escape the abuse. I closed my mind so I couldn't or wouldn't feel the abuse. I would close my eyes and take my focus off the touching." The Lord gently supported Teresa with His presence and she got in touch with more of the feelings and beliefs she had numbed out. "I hate dad. I am helpless to stop all of this. It's all my fault. I should have told mom." We continued processing these feelings and beliefs. Sometimes Teresa began to remove herself from the memory in addition to numbing out. We encouraged her to stay focused on the memory and not escape into herself as she did when the event had occurred. She was able to do this and her emotions then intensified. "[He said] I love you, Teresa," she noted. Now however, she rejected these deceptively soothing words. "How could he have done this to me? He didn't love me!" Feelings of hurt and betrayal began replacing numbness and dissociation. Her huge wall of protection slowly began to crumble, and Jesus was there to hold her as it did. Teresa began to realize how her dad's abuse had led to her reactions towards her husband during sexual intimacy.

Due to the holidays, it was three weeks before the next session. Over this break Teresa saw her dad at a family event and wondered if he had experienced any change through his own therapy. She realized he was still not truly sorry for what he did to her. In fact, she felt he didn't even care. "[All] he got was a slap on the wrist and now his life goes on." Since dad's happiness triggered Teresa's emotions, we prayerfully explored her thoughts. "Dad is not changing! He's not sorry, there is no remorse. I feel so angry at him because I sense that sexual connection with him. Why did I let him get to me? Is it really over? Will he try again? I want things to change yet I want my [biological] family together. I want him out of the family, yet I don't." Clearly, Teresa had started experiencing another layer of repressed feelings. This showed further progress that we did not want to ignore.

In the middle sessions, TPM helped Teresa break down more of her protective wall. The Lord was slowly addressing the guardian lies that kept Teresa feeling overly responsible for her family and that kept her from fully experiencing her emotions. (Guardian lies are explained in the TPM Basic Training.) We had one session with her husband so he could understand more of where the sexual difficulties were coming from and how he could support Teresa's healing process. We were pleased to find out that there had been some improvement in the area of sexual intimacy since we started therapy. Both Teresa and her husband felt encouraged about the progress, and Teresa appeared motivated to walk through her anger and other feelings. To help her continue to do that, her homework focused on writing a letter to dad. This time Teresa was to record what she wanted from her dad as a child and what he did or not do for her.

The homework assignment and a significant brief interaction with dad over the weekend stirred Teresa up emotionally more than we'd ever seen her in a previous session. It turned out to be a key healing moment. For the first time, Teresa described how nervous and scared she currently got when her dad was around. She was afraid of what he may do to her. We supported Teresa and entered the Theophostic process, focusing on the feelings of fear, uneasiness and anxiety, along with a feeling of tightness in her chest. We asked the Lord to take her where He wanted her to go and Teresa drifted to a memory of when she was 8 years old. "I felt these same feelings when dad was around and mom was gone. It is a matter of time before he finds me [and then abuses me]." We prayed for Jesus to give Teresa the strength to go through the memory without raising her protective wall. He did. "I feel bitter about everything. Why didn't mom know? As a teen I became sexually promiscuous. He [dad] caused everything!"

We asked Jesus (the Holy Spirit) to reveal His truth to Teresa in whatever way He chose. In her heart and mind she heard Jesus speak to her, "It is okay. It is not your fault. You aren't responsible . . . You can't go back and change it." The Lord also surprised her by speaking to another important area of her experience: "You need to forgive yourself." We often find that

Jesus addresses key areas our clients hadn't anticipated in Theophostic prayer. All of us realized this was an important breakthrough session.

The Lord's spoken truths now opened Teresa up to deal with another person—mom. Teresa currently felt concerned for mom because mom was dealing with so much since finding out about all the abuse. Interestingly, Teresa did not see how much mom neglected her in childhood. She had yet to confront mom about her part in the abuse. It would seem quite naïve to think that sexual abuse could continue for so many years and her mom would never have some idea about what was going on. In the prayer time, more of these feelings started to emerge for Teresa, and her homework centered on writing a letter to mom about what mom did wrong in Teresa's life. Again, the letter was a therapy letter and not for mom's eyes.

The nineteen points in Teresa's letter to mom centered around neglect and abandonment. "I was just there on the back burner. I was always left out. She really didn't care what I did as long as I was out of the way. I was always the little sister, who could never accomplish anything." Now, Teresa wanted to be treated as an adult daughter and not as a small child. Theophostic prayer had peeled away another layer. Teresa left the session more resolved to deal with issues around her mom.

Between illness, no transportation, and vacation, there was a three-week gap

between sessions. Teresa informed us that she presently had mixed feelings towards her mom. As we entered a prayer time we all sensed Teresa needed to explore her feelings and beliefs towards her mom. "I feel I am not important to her. She doesn't love me as much as she loves everyone else. There must be something wrong with me." She had memories of mom and dad attending her brother's baseball games but not her own volleyball games. Everyone else got a television for high school graduation, but she did not. Teresa's parents didn't even attend her college graduation. Memories of her teenage rebellious years then surfaced. Teresa realized that in all her rebellion, her mom never once asked her why she was doing it. Powerful beliefs fueled Teresa's anguish: "I'm all alone . . . I feel like the invisible child." As sometimes happens, the session ended before we could fully process these emotions and beliefs in the presence of Jesus. We asked the Lord to minister to Teresa, holding the wounded parts of her heart, and revealing His truth as He saw fit until our next session. For homework, Teresa was to record her anger towards mom and any other situations involving mom that arose during the week.

Due to several circumstances, we next met three weeks later. However, God answered our prayer and continued working over that time. Teresa was faithful in journaling and was now applying Theophostic herself. In this session, Teresa stated, "I feel mom's denial is mom's problem." In fact, Teresa had new motivation to speak further with her dad. Theophostic prayer had strengthened her to the point that she wanted to confront him more personally about the abuse. She had a clear sense that God was with her in this desire. We responded by prayerfully working with her on what she wanted to get out of that session.

Ever since Teresa had originally revealed the abuse to her family, her dad had voluntarily been in treatment. This is <u>very</u> unusual in an incest family unless legally required. We notified her dad's therapist to see if he felt Teresa's father was at a place in therapy for a meeting with his daughter. If everyone was prepared, the meeting would be in three weeks. The therapist was invited to attend the session along with dad.

The session with Teresa and her dad began. The Lord had been convicting him of his sin against her. As Teresa expressed her anger, hurt, and questions for him, he sincerely responded.

She felt a great release of pain and agony. For the first time, she sensed her dad accepting her as a daughter. The road to healing between father and daughter had begun.

Getting the Secret Out

Teresa's positive experience with her family confrontation is rare. Unfortunately, research shows that most incest families actually blame the victim rather than the perpetrator of the abuse. Confronting the family therefore can be a harrowing experience, one that should involve careful prayer and discussion with a trusted professional counselor. Sometimes persons appropriately choose instead to establish clear, safe boundaries with their family versus going through what can be a re-victimizing process.

Teresa had made tremendous strides in her treatment. She was utilizing the journaling exercises and doing her own TPM. She was reporting a highly satisfactory sexual life with her husband, and her family was rallying around her giving her support. The last therapeutic session with Teresa followed shortly after the session with her dad. Through God's grace, TPM, and Teresa's courage, God had done much. Gradual yet genuine heartfelt forgiveness had emerged towards her dad. Teresa shared that she no longer had a hard time dealing with the abuse that occurred between her dad and her. She realized the abuse was not her fault and that she was not responsible for her reactions to the abuse, such as keeping it a secret. "Family members are responsible for their own response to this abuse," she noted. She stated that the meeting with her dad had been the final point in removing the dark cloud that hung over her life. We all felt this was a good place to stop treatment. We would check in with Teresa in three months to see how she was doing.

At the three-month follow up session, Teresa reported healthy sexual intimacy with her husband, no depression, and no anxiety. Her family life with her parents had also changed drastically. Mom now called and visited more often. They now openly discussed the abuse and were much closer. Dad seemed to respect the relational boundaries that Teresa has established with him and he had continued in his own healing journey.

Testing Results

As seen in the above, Teresa had noted significant improvements in sexual intimacy with her husband. Her testing results also showed clear decreases in psychological distress, depression, and anxiety levels. She also decreased in the number of dysfunctional beliefs she held about herself and others, and she improved in her sense of spiritual well-being. All of these results were maintained three months later. The graphs below portray these findings. Decreasing scores reflect improvement in the first four graphs, and increasing scores on the last graph (the SWBS) reflect improvement on that instrument.

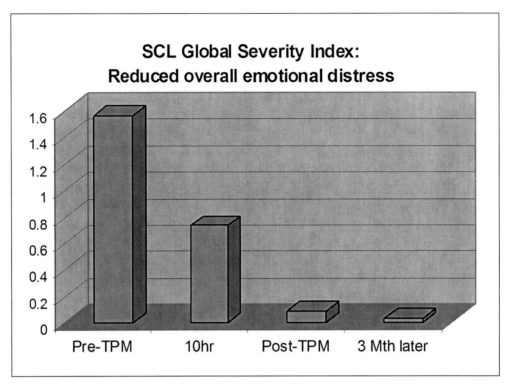

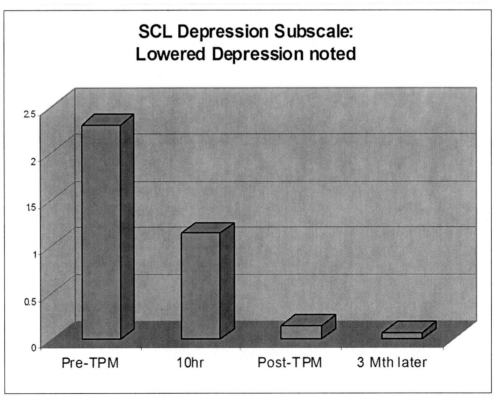

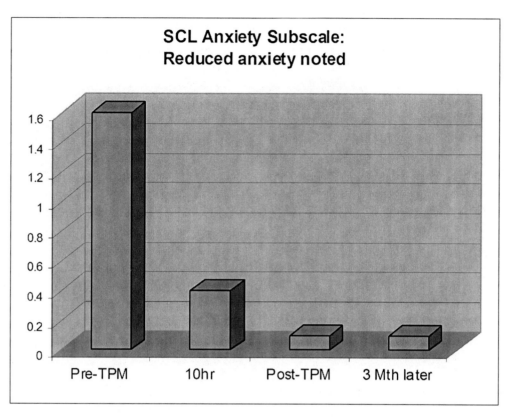

SCL Anxiety Subscale:
Reduced anxiety noted

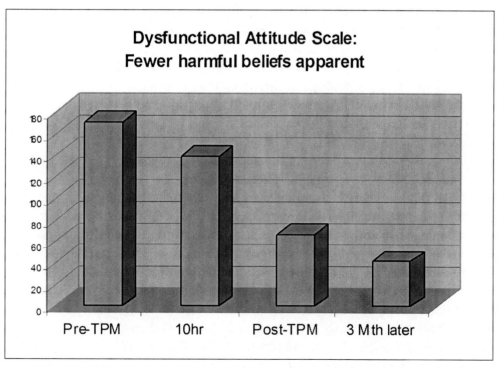

Dysfunctional Attitude Scale:
Fewer harmful beliefs apparent

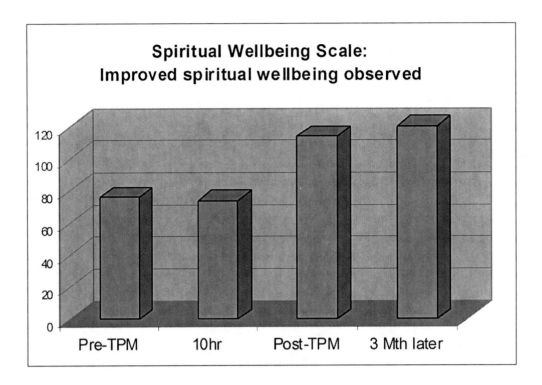

Spiritual Wellbeing Scale:
Improved spiritual wellbeing observed

External Reviewer's Assessment

Teresa's client satisfaction ratings were very high and Myrna's therapist ratings of Teresa's improvement were also positive; however, getting an objective third party to evaluate her treatment, especially someone who does not use TPM, was important in determining whether she'd truly improved. A licensed mental health professional fitting that description interviewed Teresa, reviewed her records, and asked her questions related to her symptoms. After this assessment, the reviewer noted that much symptom reduction had occurred and that she would consider Teresa to no longer have a mental illness.

Discussion

Teresa clearly had a positive experience in her treatment. She showed great courage in facing painful events and difficult feelings. Once the shock of realizing what had happened wore off, her family also responded well to her limit setting and confrontations of dad. As noted previously, this is an unusual occurrence. Most often, abuse victims are chronically blamed and re-victimized by their families, with the perpetrator instead being let off the hook. Now, Teresa appears to have recovered and is moving on in her life. We rejoice in her over-coming victory!

Myrna and Annette masterfully combined TPM and sound clinical strategies (journaling, meeting with the spouse, dad, etc.) to the benefit of their client. Indeed, I (Fernando) am glad Teresa was seeing such compassionate, well-trained people. It's important to know our limits. Many people lack the training to deal with such an extensive abuse history. In such cases, we recommend referring to a mental health professional familiar with TPM and standard sexual abuse treatments.

About the Treating Ministers

Myrna Thatcher is a Licensed Marriage and Family Therapist in the Cottonwood, Idaho region. Annette Smith is a highly skilled lay counselor that works with Myrna as a co-counselor and intercessory prayer partner. Together, they have the ministry, AbbaDaddy House. They can be reached at (208) 962-7384 or abbadaddyhouse@isp.com.

Chapter Four References

1. Foa, Edna & Keene, Terence (2000). Effective Treatments for PTSD: Practice Guidelines from the International Society for Traumatic Stress Studies. New York: Guilford

Chapter 5:

Christine's "Song of Solomon"

Pauline Burthwick, Ph.D, MSW, LICSW in collaboration with Mike and Deana
Woytasek (lay prayer ministers), and Fernando Garzon, Psy.D.

*The Song of Solomon is a beautiful book in the Bible that describes the romantic love
of a man and woman in the covenant of marriage. While Christine knew logically that
God sanctions physical intimacy in marriage, she could not truly enjoy it until the lies
she believed about such intimacy were healed. This is her story.*

A Word about the Setting

Unlike the other cases you've read so far, Christine sought emotional healing through her
local church. She was assigned to a married couple as her lay prayer ministers, and this
couple was under the supervision of a mental health professional that oversees the organized
caregiving ministries in Christine's church. The lay ministers had received basic and advanced
training in Theophostic prayer and had well over 100 hours of experience in this form of
prayer.

Normally, sessions lasted two to three hours in this lay setting since there is no concern
with billing issues. The lay ministers were not acting in the capacity of counselors, but rather
as non-professional prayer facilitators.

This case was written by a clinical social worker who collaborates with trained lay persons
in ministering Theophostic prayer. We hope that you will be encouraged by the collaboration
in the body of Christ to bring emotional healing to hurting people.

Christine's Dilemma

"If we can't have sex, the marriage is over!" Such was the ominous statement of Christine's
husband about their difficulties. Christine, a 40-year-old White woman, had been married for
five years but now her marriage was clearly on the rocks. Unlike other persons we (Mike and
Deana) work with who normally suffer from a variety of causes to anxiety and depression symptoms, Christine's chief problem was very focused. She was having difficulties in engaging in

sexual relations with her husband. Such a problem can have many different sources. Christine's first session gave us clear clues about her particular instance.

Within a few months of getting married, Christine's current problems started. During intercourse, she would experience anxiety, flashbacks of childhood sexual abuse incidents, and sexual "shut-down". She tried to ask her husband to refrain from touching her in certain ways that seemed to trigger the flashbacks, but he did not appear to understand the connection and refused to do so. Later we would discover why he reacted this way. Christine also tried praying and self-talk (For example: "I know that this is my husband, this is O.K. I am pure in God's sight. It is O.K. Please help me Lord."). These were initially helpful and made physical intimacy tolerable for the first couple of years, but eventually they no longer assisted her. She then tried "stuffing it" again, pretending she was O.K. and just tried to endure sex, but that did not work either. The subsequent stress and marital difficulties over these problems overwhelmed Christine. She heard about Theophostic prayer from two women she prayed with weekly. Now she was coming to see us feeling depressed and yet with a glimmer of hope that God could heal her. Christine had never sought any mental health services in the past. She would eventually have four two-hour prayer sessions with us.

Christine's Story

Christine's parents (51 years married) are now professing Christians in the Baptist tradition, but during her growing up years they were doing anything but living a Christian lifestyle. Their relationship was always conflictual. Christine saw her mother as loving, nurturing, and supportive; however, she viewed her father as "controlling and very critical." She wondered if he really loved her. She had a sister, Sandy, who was two years older, and a brother, Ron, four years older. Christine reported good relationships with both Sandy and Ron.

When Christine was about five, her family moved from California to the Midwest. With this change, her dad began working nights and was at home sleeping during the days. Christine described him as becoming more critical of her from this early time on. She did however have other male influences in her life that seemed more supportive.

Sadly however, one of them proved treacherous. He was Uncle John, a man that she innocently liked and trusted. When Christine was in the 5th grade, Uncle John sexually abused her four times. Three instances occurred in his home and the fourth at his cabin. The last incident, in the cabin, also involved her sister. Though the abuse fell short of intercourse, it resulted in turmoil for Christine from then on and led to the current presenting symptoms. Christine and her sister did not tell their parents about the abuse and there was a sense on Christine's part that her parents failed to protect her and her sister.

Christine made an initial profession of faith at age 12, but she often felt "too dirty" for God. In the sixth grade, she started rebelling, perhaps in response to her father's criticisms and her abuse experiences. As she got into Junior and Senior High School, arguments with her father were frequent. She maintained good grades, but began partying, using drugs, drinking, and having sex. Her grades helped her to hide these behaviors until she could find a way to leave the home.

In her junior year of high school, Christine succeeded in moving out of the house and into an apartment with a friend to "escape from her dad". She worked at a restaurant and eventually met a very friendly 40-year-old married man (Sam) with children around her age. He always came in and visited with her. Indeed, she grew to trust in his kindness. As soon as she turned 18, he surprised her by asking her out. Christine accepted, based on his caring attitude. He bought her things, took her places, and treated her relatively well. At first, she believed that he loved her and she felt as if she loved him.

At age 19, she became pregnant by Sam and had an abortion at his insistence. During that time, she did not know or consider that the baby might be a life. She continued in this enmeshed relationship for about 8 more years. Indeed, every time she tried to end the relationship, she took Sam back. Why? He skillfully played to her sympathies. For example, during one break-up he said that he just had a friend die in his arms (so she couldn't leave him now!). Another time he said that he had just been diagnosed with a terminal illness. The list goes on.

When Christine was 28, her sister-in-law shared the Gospel with her and she recommitted her life to Christ. After this, she stopped having a sexual relationship with Sam, but believed she should stay in relationship with him to "win him to Christ." Slowly, she saw that her efforts were failing so she discussed her concerns with her pastor. "Should I stay with him to try and convert him or end the relationship?" she asked. Of course, the pastor strongly advised ending the relationship! After a while she was able to do so with this encouragement and the support of her church.

Two years after breaking up with Sam (when Christine was 31), she attended one of Neil Anderson's *Freedom in Christ* conferences. At the conference, she began considering how her childhood participation with her cousins in occult activities (using the Quija board, fortune telling, and tarot cards), as well as her experiences of sexual abuse may have been affecting her. Even at this time she felt anger, shame, and fear of seeing the perpetrator somewhere. During the conference she had an individual Freedom Appointment (using Anderson's *Steps to Freedom*). This was an intense ministry time for her. She reported, "I forgave both my dad and the man who molested me. I was only able to do it after five intensive days of learning [at the conference] about forgiveness and how important it would be for me to forgive. It took me about six hours to actually get through all the forgiveness. It made a significant difference in my life. The fear and anger were gone, and I thought I was healed of all of it." Indeed, the conference and appointment did appear to help Christine in many areas. Her current sexual dysfunction went unnoticed because she was not sexually active after her recommitment to Christ until after she got married. The renewed physical intimacy served as a trigger to signal God wanted to do more healing in her life.

Christine continued growing in her church and eventually felt called to spend two years in missions work overseas. While there, she met her future husband who was also involved in mission work. Shortly after completing their overseas term, they returned to the United States and got married. Although her husband knew about the abuse, Christine did not at first share with him about the flashbacks. This was because her self-talk and prayers were initially helping her cope. The flashbacks became noticeably worse about three years into the marriage. This was particularly troublesome because it was at a time when they were beginning to become actively involved with ministry to married couples. When she then told her husband about the flashbacks, she received his negative response.

Her husband's lack of understanding caused Christine to feel re-victimized. Christine has since learned, as her husband has gone on to receive his own healing, that his response to her problem was actually due to unhealed wounds and lies believed from his first failed marriage ("This once perfect marriage is doomed.") and from childhood ("I'm doomed").

Christine's Prayer Sessions

First Session

We met Christine and bonded with her through listening compassionately to her story. Christine had many feelings stirred up, and she had previously read the materials we had given her describing Theophostic Prayer. We waited for the right time to ask the Lord's direction. Eventually, it came. Christine was tearful and ready to receive.

We prayed, "Lord Jesus, we ask you to give Christine the grace and courage to go to the place you want her to go today?" Christine's expression notably changed.

"What are you feeling, Christine?"

"Fear and confusion," she responded. "I'm ten years old and in the living room. Uncle John has sat down beside me. He's talking with me but I don't feel safe. I'm nervous. He's starting to touch me. He asked, 'Has anyone done this for you before?' I said 'No' and felt like what he was doing was wrong. I wondered if he was going to stop."

As Christine experienced the memory, she also expressed shame and embarrassment. She felt bad for not telling her parents. At this point, we wanted to start discerning the lies she was believing. "Christine," we asked, "why were you feeling 'bad'?"

"I did something to provoke this. It is my fault." Christine then focused in the memory on the perpetrator, her uncle. "Uncle John was always someone I could trust. Why did he turn on me?!...It is my fault because it continued and it had to be kept a secret – I should have told anyway."

"Lord, would You reveal Your truth to Christine?" Instead of her receiving truth Christine drifted to a memory picture of when her uncle asked her parents if she and her sister could go up North with him to his cabin. He said his wife was already up there. Christine felt fear and dread as she viewed this memory. She also grew angry with her parents for sending her up there.

"Why did they send me up there?!" She moaned. "I have been kicking myself over the years for not telling my parents."

Next, she spontaneously drifted to a memory picture of bedtime at the cabin. We followed. The cabin seemed dark and the forest very scary. Fear and panic filled her as she wondered how far he would go. He put both Christine and her sister Sandy in the bed with him, one on each side of him. He took turns fondling them. "It seemed to go on for hours...I was afraid he was going to hurt Sandy."

We invited Jesus presence. "Lord Jesus, Christine is feeling like it's her fault, she should have stopped it, he's going to hurt Sandy. Would You reveal Your truth to Christine in whatever way You choose?"

"He's here," Christine stated, "But I can't get to Him." At this time, Christine asked a profound question that sometimes surfaces in ministry to sexual abuse victims.

"Why didn't Jesus stop this? Why did He let it go on?"

We knew better than to naively try to answer such a profoundly painful question. Mistimed theological explanations don't satisfy today's hurting hearts much as they didn't satisfy Job in the Bible. Instead, we often find that Jesus will respond to such questions Himself. When He does, His responses are infinitely better and wiser than anything we could have answered.[1]

"Lord Jesus, what is it you want her to know about why You didn't stop it?" We asked. "Christine," we cautioned, "don't try to 'figure it out', just listen with your heart and see if you get a sense of a response. If nothing happens, that's okay; we'll deal with that, too." She paused.

"Jesus is trying to tell me that He cared, He was there. It is not [my] fault. Man is fallen and sinful, what he [Uncle John] did was wrong…[I] did not know the right thing to do." Christine then reported feeling the arms of Jesus around her holding her. We rejoiced at what the Lord was doing. As we checked her beliefs, there was increased peace; however, she still believed she was a "little bit dirty." Then Jesus continued to minister to her. She sensed Jesus continuing to hold her and to stroke her hair. He said, "It is OK, you are not dirty." Christine basked in Jesus presence for a time while we quietly prayed and thanked God for what He was doing.

As the session drew to a close, we did a check on today's work. "Christine, scan through the memories we've covered today and see how they feel. Are they all peaceful and calm?"

"I feel more peaceful and encouraged, but there's still some uneasiness." Based on her response, we knew progress had been made, but there was more work to be done. However, Christine did feel stronger. She had a clear sense at the end of the prayer time that she now wanted to tell her parents about what had happened. She did this later in the week, resulting in a very positive experience. Uncle John had since divorced Christine's aunt, so a direct family confrontation of him did not take place; however, much healing occurred through her parents' response to her disclosure. We unfortunately find such responses an exception rather than the rule when someone discloses sexual abuse.

Splinter Lies

Splinter lies are lies that were not felt or understood the first time through the memory because the relief was so great from the initial truth received that the person is unable to feel any remaining negative emotions in the memory event.[2]

Second Session

We usually start the second session by reviewing the memories that presented during the first session. In Christine's case, this was very important since there was some improvement, but the memories weren't entirely "peaceful and calm" at the end. We wondered if Splinter Lies might be present.

Christine was anxious about going back to check the memory in the cabin. We quietly prayed and proclaimed Christ's victory over all the strategies the enemy might use to impede her ministry experience. This prayer freed Christine to be able to overcome her hesitancy to go back to the memory in the cabin.

As she viewed the memory picture, Christine wondered why she felt she could not come into contact with Jesus.

"This works for others, not for me. If Jesus was there, why did He allow this?" She again wondered.

"These are good questions, Christine. Lord, what would You respond to these questions?" We asked. As Christine waited on His response, she began feeling a sense of His warmth.

Christine stated, "Jesus is telling me that sometimes bad things happen to good people, but it is not His will." She felt peace at His response, and was then ready to go back to the cabin memory when she was on the bed with Sandy and Uncle John. We praised the Lord for His response, for she needed to hear it from Him, and then she could freely choose wholeheartedly to view the memory.

Christine now goes into the memory picture and immediately finds herself in the presence of the Lord. We were silent for a long time during this marvelous work of the Holy Spirit, so we will just give you what she told us as she kept us informed of what was happening in her mind.

Christine senses peace. "It's like we are there, but we won't be hurt anymore. Jesus is holding me in his arms. He cares for me...He wants to tell me it is O.K. He is rocking me in His arms. He loves me. He said it is terrible what happened to me, but it is over now. It is time to look at it, embrace what happened, but realize it is finished, it is over. The Lord will not allow it to keep hurting me any longer. He wants me to release all my pain to Him. It is true, it all happened, but it is finished. Satan meant this for evil and to destroy the child [in me], but Jesus redeemed me. When He redeemed me and washed me of all my sin, the filth of what had happened to me was washed away too. I am not dirty any more." We noted Christine appeared to have deep conviction in her heart about this now.

"He keeps saying that His blood has washed it all away and I am clean. I am not dirty any more. I am redeemed. He has rescued me out of darkness and I am washed clean and pure. He is sorry for all the years of anguish I had over this. He wants me to know that He has given me much to make up for what the locusts have eaten."

"Jesus saved me and gave me new life. He sent me on the mission field and gave me my husband. He is saying, 'Your husband is different than this man [Uncle John]. He [your husband] is a godly wonderful man who loves you very much. Jesus has given us our marriage and it is good, perfect and holy in His eyes. Our courtship was pure and our marriage bed is clean and undefiled. This is the good and perfect marriage that the Lord ordained. This is how it is supposed to be. Our lovemaking is pure. There is nothing to be afraid of. It is not happening anymore. Our lovemaking is completely different from the past evil and darkness."

"I see the picture of salvation, of being in Jesus arms, complete with radiant light in place of all the evil and darkness. I now have a wonderful, godly husband who loves me. When we make love, it is because we love each other and God says it is good. Jesus said it was not my fault; I was a child and had nothing to do with it. It was something done to me and God is calling me to let go of the shame. It was not my fault for not telling either. I did not know that I should have told. I need to leave my sister in His arms. I was not responsible for what happened to Sandy. The same evil man who abused me, abused her also. She was a victim as I was, it happened to both of us. I do not have to be afraid anymore. The evil man is gone and it is all over. I am safe now and it is OK. I am with the Lord now." We marveled at how deeply and completely the Lord's words went into Christine's soul, compared to what we might have offered.

Free Will

Jesus will not violate the free will of the one receiving prayer. He will never require a person to go to a memory they do not want to face or re-visit. TPM prayer facilitators will not ask or require that either. Instead, the facilitator takes every question or objection to Jesus so that He might reveal His perspective for each one. Once the prayer recipient receives the Lord's perspective, their fears and doubts subside and they often are ready to continue in prayer. If they choose not to, this is respected.

Making Suggestions

It is important to be aware that during a Theophostic prayer session, consistent with Smith's (2007) Theophostic Prayer Ministry Guidelines,[3] the facilitators are not interpreting the memory or making suggestions about what happened or suggesting specific "truth" that should replace the misbeliefs. Everything that presents is placed before Jesus, the One who is Truth, for His interpretation and Word of Truth on the matter and the one receiving prayer reports to the facilitators what they are hearing, seeing, sensing, and feeling (both physical and emotional feelings). It is also important to note that all truth that is received during the session is coming from the Holy Spirit even though most people tend to relate to the person of Jesus during a session.

We sat in holy awe at what God was doing. Christine cried, thinking about Sandy and how her sister has been hurt and has rejected the Lord. Christine senses Sandy's pain and spontaneously prays about this. The Lord then gave her a sense that Sandy would come back in time. Christine should be patient, love her and wait. As Christine received this hope, the pain lifted off her, and the Lord now carried it.

At the end of this prayer time, Christine wanted to pray a prayer of forgiveness from her heart to release Uncle John fully into the Lord's hands and to forgive her parents for not protecting her. Christine did this, and our time ended with prayers to break any one-flesh soul ties with Uncle John that may have been forged in the abuse. In memories like these we were working on, we often find this form of prayer removes any "legal right" for demonic oppression to remain attached to the past episodes. After the session, we both felt this was a breakthrough for Christine. We wondered what her report would be next week.

Third Session

In our next session, Christine reported that she was able to engage in sexual intimacy with her husband without any flashbacks, anxiety, or discomfort. She actually enjoyed it. Praise the Lord! We celebrated together.

With Christine's key concern resolved, we asked if she would like to work on anything else. We had seen plenty of things in Christine's history that might need work, but we wanted to respect her desires. Christine stated she would like to continue working on some other areas, and reported a recent occurrence which was a "triggering event". She was fixing coffee and her husband said, "It needs more cream." This caused her very strong emotions of hurt and upset.

We had her focus on these feelings. "I know my emotions are way out of line with what was going on in the situation," she observed.

"We understand, Christine. What were you believing that fueled the hurt and upset?"

"I did it wrong. I am not good enough."

We asked the Lord to bring to mind what He wanted her to know about this or to take her where He wanted her to go. A memory came up of when she made something for her mom for last year's Mother's day. Her dad's response to her was, "Why didn't you do something different?" She felt frustrated and angry and believed, "I am not good enough, I ruined it, No matter what I do, it is not good enough."

Keeping her focused on the emotions of this event, she drifted to a memory picture of her 7th grade report card. We followed. She had gotten all A's, but her dad's response was, "Why aren't these A+'s?"

"Dad's not happy with it," Christine noted, "I couldn't do anything about it, I will never be able to please dad, I am not good enough, I am a disappointment to dad. Why should I try?"

Christine felt hurt. We encouraged her to embrace this pain and asked Jesus to reveal His truth to her.

"I sense God says it is not my fault. My dad's disappointment was not about me, but about himself. God says, 'It was good enough for Me. I was pleased with you. You don't have to measure up to the world's standards.'"

Focusing on the emotion of not feeling loved by her dad, she explained that when she was young, up to about age 5, her dad adored her, but when she began to have her own identity, she felt he no longer accepted her. As she focused on the rejection and upset she felt from not being loved, she remembered a time when she was 12 that her dad slapped her at the dinner table and shouted at her. We explored the memory for lies.

"Dad will only love me if I do not say anything he does not like. I must be perfect and have no thoughts of my own," she noted.

"Lord, what would You reveal to Christine about these thoughts?" We petitioned.

"The Lord is saying, He [Jesus] loved me, He cared for me, He knew I would grow up and accept Him."

Focusing on any leftover upset feelings, another memory picture presented to her of her dad hitting and kicking her brother. Her dad was out of control and threatening her brother. Her mother and sister were afraid, and Christine, age 10 in this memory, was watching and crying. After that, she did not trust her dad because she believed "he might not stop". She felt fear, helplessness, and hatred. She believed he had to be avoided and that he did not like them.

Another memory came of Junior High and of how mean her dad was to her mother. She wished her mother would leave him and was told by her dad to "obey or else." At this point, Christine felt "stuck", so we asked the Lord what He wanted to do. Christine sensed the need to forgive her father. She then prayed, extending forgiveness toward her father for never holding her and loving her. She also felt led to forgive herself for having hatred and bitterness against him. As she prayed both of these prayers, she felt the pain being lifted off and the burden going off to heaven with God.

The Multi-layered Aspects of Forgiveness

As this incident points out, forgiveness is often multi-layered. Christine had forgiven her father in the last session for not protecting her, but she had not recognized her anger at him in other areas until this session. The clutter of unforgiveness and self-condemnation (the need for self-forgiveness) were important areas to address in prayer for this session.

Session Four

Christine's final prayer session consisted of reviewing all the memories that had presented in the previous session to ensure that all of the memories were peaceful and calm. The memory in the cabin was reviewed and all was peaceful and calm. When the memory of the first sexual abuse event was reviewed, there was some anxiety and confusion around the question Uncle John had asked ("Has anyone ever done this for you before?") She felt terrible about what he was doing, but he made it sound good. Then she heard from the Lord, "It was not good. He was wrong. You are not there anymore. You are O.K." After this, Christine reported that she felt peaceful in every memory. No other emotional concerns were identified and we determined that the prayer sessions were completed.

Christine's Results

Christine's presenting problem was very specific and focused; thus, her SCL 90R testing scores prior to treatment reflected little distress. Throughout her counseling and at the 3-month follow-up, all her scores were below levels of clinical concern.

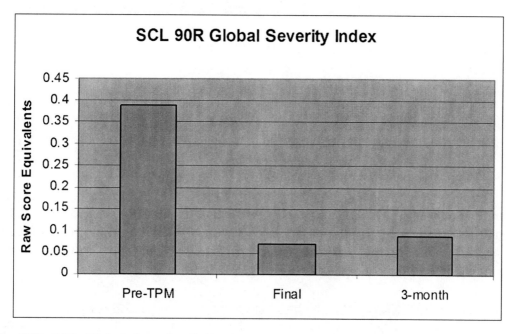

The SCL 90R Global Severity Scale demonstrated normal range functioning at each testing interval. The DAS also reflected scores within the normal range prior to and throughout treatment.

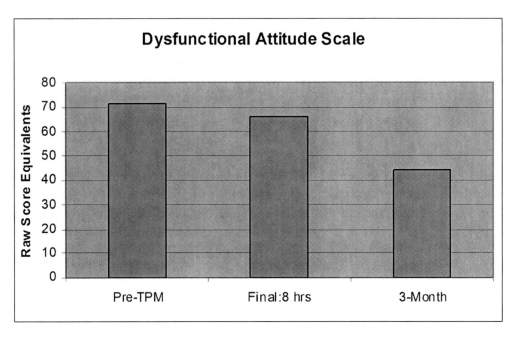

Dysfunctional Attitude Scale

Given these scoring patterns, how do we know if this ministry method really helped Christine? Since Christine's issue was very specific (sexual dysfunction), it seems appropriate to examine this area in line with what Smith identifies as his fourfold test of mind renewal. He outlines the following four indicators in his 2007 edition basic training manual. (p. 161 - 164).

How do the "Four Indicators" line up with Christine's session outcomes?

1. <u>Is the truth the recipient received during the ministry session consistent with biblical truth?</u>

   Nothing Christine sensed in prayer appeared to contradict scripture.

2. <u>Does the recipient experience the perfect peace of Christ in the resolved memory(ies)?</u>

   When the person returns to thinking about the memories that were previously painful, they experience the memory as a historical fact yet their emotions are peaceful and calm when TPM is successful. One year after her ministry sessions, Christine continues to report that the memories that were worked on are no longer interfering with her life (See #4 for further details of this one year follow-up). The flashbacks stopped after the second prayer session.

3. <u>Does the recipient have genuine compassion and forgiveness for the offender(s)?</u>

   When there is true and complete healing, the one healed willingly forgives the perpetrator. Sometimes it takes time to get to that point if there were many instances of abuse. This forgiveness enables the client to move on with life and make responsible decisions on what to do. In some cases, confrontation may be necessary to stop an abuser who is still abusing. The Lord directs and leads each one in this area. Christine was able to forgive her perpetrator. In her situation, the abuser divorced her relative and she no longer has the occasion or reason to see him. In addition, she no longer has a fear of meeting him somewhere or feels the need to be constantly "on guard" in case she would run into him sometime either.

4. Does the ministry result in genuine transformation and life change?

Prior to receiving Theophostic prayer, Christine would use self-talk and prayer during times of sexual intimacy with her husband to try to endure it and get through the flashbacks. This took a great deal of self-effort. She knew cognitively the truth that this was her husband and that it was O.K. for her to receive his love. In fact, she told herself those very same logical truths repeatedly during times of sexual intimacy. Having that "head" knowledge of the truth was not enough to remove the flashbacks or to enable her to enjoy relating sexually to her husband whom she loved and who loved her very much. She had to have heart knowledge through the mind renewal prayer of TPM.

We (Mike & Deana) followed up with Christine one year after her ministry sessions. She is still reporting satisfaction in her sexual relationship with her husband. Her husband likewise confirms this result. Indeed, Christine reports that her marriage has been restored. The duration of this change is much longer than the three-month follow-up data that we've reported in the other cases, so I (Fernando) believe it is meaningful. Granted that this is only a relative measure of "permanence", but the length of time with symptom remission is very positive in terms of psychological research. Another positive aspect of this particular case is the length of time it took to achieve this result. Christine received healing from this problem in three and ½ hours (by the end of the second session) of prayer and continued to work on other issues for the remaining two sessions. As can be seen with Karen's case (chapter two), the amount of TPM sessions needed can vary.

What would have happened if Christine's problem hadn't improved with the help of these lay counselors? In their regular supervision sessions, the counselors would have discussed the situation and a referral to a Christian therapist experienced in sex therapy would have been made. This is one reason that we believe supervision and consultation relationships with Christian mental health professionals are so important for lay counselors. Such professionals can help identify when other resources are needed.

Christine and her husband have gone on to become trained lay Theophostic prayer ministers. The training process required each of them to receive ten hours of prayer and facilitate 30 hours of prayer to be able to take the advanced level Theophostic training. During the additional ministry "practice" times, Christine reported healing and forgiveness for issues related to having the abortion. She also continues working on the impact her critical father has had on her life. Changes that she has observed with her father are that she no longer feels triggered and upset by his comments. She notes, "I can overlook it and not get upset, because I do not feel the hurt since the lies are gone."

As previously mentioned, Christine's husband has received healing for issues around his own childhood and his first marriage that ended in divorce. Christine was the prayer partner in these sessions for her husband and now she has much greater understanding about why he reacted the way he did when she was having her difficulties. He was responding out of underlying lies and emotions from his past that were driving his reactions. The couple now has much greater emotional intimacy as well as physical intimacy since they have greater empathy for each other's experience.

Conclusions with Christine's Case

When Christine started treatment with Mike and Deana, she knew Biblical passages like the Song of Solomon that highlight the sanctioned place of romantic love in the covenant of marriage. This knowledge was not enough to permit her to enjoy such an experience until the Author of that sacred book ministered His grace to her in prayer times. Christine could now live out her own "Song of Solomon" with her husband.

"Does Theophostic work?" Christine would give a resounding "Yes!" to that question. What is the evidence? She has freedom! She no longer has flashbacks when she has intimacy with her husband. She no longer has to pray and do self-talk during sexual relations because Jesus entered her experiences at age eleven. She has a testimony! Jesus brought her His truth experientially, and enabled her to "know" in her deepest parts the truth that it was not her fault, that she is not with that other man anymore, and that it is good to have intimacy with her husband who loves her. Christine reports, "If that memory comes to mind now, there is no pain. I see the Lord and hear the truths He spoke to me." She uses the now living, personal Word that He spoke to her in her sessions to refute the enemy of her soul, just like Jesus did to defeat Satan when he was tempted in the wilderness.

As I (Pauline) have watched Jesus minister to many through Theophostic prayer, I see Him preparing a table before the one receiving prayer, I see Him restoring their soul in the presence of their enemy. He brings the receiver to a place of green pastures and quiet waters where their cup overflows. Sound familiar?

> The LORD is my shepherd; I shall not be in want. He makes me lie down in green pastures, he leads me beside quiet waters, he restores my soul. He guides me in paths of righteousness for his name's sake. Even though I walk through the valley of the shadow of death, I will fear no evil, for you are with me; your rod and your staff, they comfort me. You prepare a table before me in the presence of my enemies. You anoint my head with oil; my cup overflows. Surely goodness and love will follow me all the days of my life, and I will dwell in the house of the LORD forever. (Psalm 23, NIV)

Comparing Teresa's Case (Chapter 4) and Christine's Case

While Teresa and Christine both had sexual intimacy difficulties with their husbands, they were very different in other areas. For example, Teresa's history of sexual abuse was much more extensive, leading to more severe anxiety and depression symptoms related to the abuse than Christine's symptoms. Teresa's father (someone very involved in her upbringing) was her perpetrator and Teresa continued to have regular contact with him, while Christine's perpetrator (Uncle John) was a person much less involved in her life and now he has left her social environment entirely. The complexities of Teresa's case led to additional interventions orchestrated by her therapist and a longer course of treatment than in Christine's case. Teresa and Christine's stories highlight that each sexual abuse survivor is unique. As noted in Teresa's case, we were glad she was working with a Christian mental health professional because of the intricacies involved in her care. Christine's case demonstrated a successful lay counseling application of Theophostic Prayer Ministry under clinical supervision.

About the Authors

Pauline Burthwick, Ph.D., MSW, is a Licensed Independent Clinical Social Worker in Minnesota and North Dakota. She has worked in Minnesota and North Dakota practicing social work both at the bachelors level and at the clinical level primarily in the service areas of chronic illness, medical social work, gerontology, mental health, and Christian Counseling. She was formerly the Program Director and a Faculty member of the Social Work Program at Concordia College in Moorhead, Minnesota. Pauline now serves the body of Christ through her local/regional ministry called Releasing Destiny. She has also been instrumental in establishing a non-profit called Releasing Destiny World Wide and has ministered in Pakistan in 2006. You may contact her at www.info@releasingdestinty.org

Michael Woytasek is a graduate of Village Schools of the Bible in Minneapolis, MN. He has served as an Elder at New Hope Church.

Deana Woytasek has a B.A. degree in Biblical Studies from American Christian College. She began working with the deeply wounded as a prayer partner in her local church.

Michael and Deana both have received Theophostic training in Basic, Advanced, and Level II Apprenticeship under Dr. Ed Smith. They've also received Life Model training under Dr. E. James Wilder. Michael and Deana enjoy working together as a lay person prayer ministry team under the supervision of a professional at New Hope Church in Minneapolis, MN

Chapter Five References

1. We should note that we are not saying that there is no place for explanations concerning evil, suffering, etc. with clients. Rather, the timing of such discussions is extremely important. When a client is in deep emotional pain, explanation is not needed as much as empathy is. The book of Job clearly suggests this. No answer will satisfy a heart in pain unless it comes from the Lord Himself.
2. Smith, E. M. (2007) *Theophostic Prayer Ministry: Basic Seminar Training Manual.* Campbellsville, KY: New Creation Publishing.
3. Smith, E. M. (2007) *Theophostic ministry guidelines.* Campbellsville, KY: New Creation Publishing

Chapter 6

What Does It All Mean?

A Summary of the Case Study Research
Fernando Garzon, Psy.D; Marian Teske, Psy.D.; David Kleinschuster, Psy.D.

Y ou've now heard the stories of Gloria, Karen, Teresa, and Christine. Clearly, they seem to have benefited from Theophostic, and their testing data supports their contention that something good has happened to them. What about the other cases and the overall results? What sorts of limitations should be considered in these results?

We'll start with the other cases and overall results. Our study included the types of clients that are most common in the outpatient psychotherapy setting—those suffering from depression conditions, anxiety conditions, or adjustment disorders. Table one below gives you an idea of the basic demographics, diagnoses, and SCL 90R GSI scores of the group. Note that not all clients answered every question, so the number (N) is noted where appropriate.

Table 1

Participant Characteristics (N=16)

Mean Age	38 (range 19 – 57)		Mean Sessions	13 (range 4 – 30)	
Gender	n		Primary Diagnosis		
Male	4	(27%)	Mood Disorder	8	(50%)
Female	11	(73%)	Anxiety Disorder	5	(31%)
			Adjustment Disorder	3	(19%)
Ethnicity					
Caucasian	12	(80%)	Denomination		
Hispanic	1	(6%)	Non-denominational	4	(31%)
Asian American	1	(6%)	Evangelical Free	4	(31%)
Multiracial	1	(6%)	Baptist	4	(31%)
			Lutheran		1 (7%)

Education

			Mean SCL-90-R GSI Scores & SD		
High School	4	(31%)			
Some College	2	(15%)	Pretreatment	1.23	+/- .43
College Degree	6	(46%)	Post-treatment	.49	+/- .41
Masters Degree	1	(8%)	3-Month Follow-up	.41	+/- .35

Since the cases involve a "mixed bag" so to speak, the best way to analyze the results is to look at the outcomes individually. Fortunately, one of the instruments, the SCL- 90R, has specific information on large samples of outpatient clients as well as on people who are not in treatment. This permits clinically meaningful comparisons. A statistical investigation like this one is called an analysis of clinical significance.[1] Derogatis and others have written specifically on how to apply clinical significance procedures with the SCL- 90R's most useful overall scale, the Global Severity Index (GSI). [2,3,4] Before we begin though, I (Fernando) must warn you:

Caution: You've about to enter "The Statistics Zone". It's that vast realm that creates panic and confusion in even the most brilliant of minds. Accordingly, we will endeavor to give you our own version of "Case Statistics for Dummies" (By the way, we often feel like some of those dummies). Citations given provide detailed information on the analysis, for those interested. Read at your own risk.

Clinical significance is very important. You've heard the old saying "You can use statistics to prove anything." Because of that, researchers have developed this type of comparison for clinical research. It's more informative and accurate than many other types of analyses, and it helps us understand just how much change took place in the study.

For the SCL-90R's GSI scale, researchers have used certain statistical procedures and developed certain cutoff scores to prevent people from misinterpreting chance improvement (measurement error) as true improvement. A table can then be made of clients who demonstrated four categories of results: Deterioration, Unchanged, Improvement (reliable improvement, that is), and Recovered.[5]

Deterioration is defined as clear evidence that the client worsened during treatment. All forms of psychotherapy inevitably lead to some outcomes that are not desired for some people. The question of course becomes how many. In typical psychotherapy research, the percentage of clients who normally would end up as deteriorated is 5-10%.[6]

The Unchanged category consists of people who went through treatment and their testing results do not indicate a change other than what might be expected from chance.[7] The number of clients who might be classified in this category differs with each psychotherapy study. Obviously, the lower the number, like in the Deterioration category, the better.

The Improvement category indicates that there has been a statistically reliable positive change in the client that goes beyond the chance measurement error fluctuations found in the testing instrument.[8] The more people in a study that demonstrate "Improvement", the better. A researcher can have more confidence that something good happened for the client in the treatment when someone is classified in this category.

The Recovered category, as the name implies, is the best category of all. In essence, this category indicates there's a high probability that the client is now experiencing such low symptom levels that they are much like people who are not in psychotherapy.[9] It's very likely that any symptoms they have are in the normal range. Like the Improved category, the more people fitting this category the better.

Let's take a look at a table of the classifications that arose from this research. Outpatient stands for the people seen by licensed therapists. "LC" stands for people seen by lay counselors. Note: These cases are not presented in the same sequence as discussed in the chapters of the book.

Table 2

Pretreatment, Post-treatment and 3-Month Follow-up SCL-90-R GSI Scores

Client	Group	Pre	Post	Outcome	3 Month	3 Month Outcome
1	Outpatient	.80	.50	Unchanged	.48	Unchanged
2	Outpatient	1.70	.13	Recovered	.13	Recovered
3	Outpatient	1.39	.39	Recovered	.17	Recovered
4	Outpatient	1.43	.19	Recovered	.19	Recovered
5	Outpatient	1.40	.34	Recovered	.14	Recovered
6	Outpatient	1.44	.80	Improved	.84	Improved
7	Outpatient	1.56	.08	Recovered	.03	Recovered
8	Outpatient	1.00	.10	Recovered	.08	Recovered
9	Outpatient	.76	1.66	Deteriorated	1.07	Unchanged
10	Outpatient	1.33	.80	Improved	1.10	Unchanged
11	Outpatient	.66	.00	Recovered	.00	Recovered
12	Outpatient	1.26	.68	Improved	.53	Recovered
13	Outpatient	.90	.58	Recovered	.94	Unchanged
14	LC	.83	.48	Recovered	.28	Recovered
15	LC	2.21	.43	Recovered	.24	Recovered
16	LC	1.08	.54	Recovered	.13	Recovered

SCL-90-R = Symptom Checklist 90 – Revised
GSI = Global Severity Index
LC = Lay counseling client

At post-treatment, we can see that thirteen out of sixteen participants (81%) reported meaningful positive change (Improved or Recovered). Only one person's results (7%) was classified as Deteriorated. Comparing post-treatment and the three month follow-up results, we can also see that treatment gains were maintained in most cases. The one deteriorated case also reduced to the Unchanged category at the 3 month follow-up. Only two participants lost their gains. Case 11 results were likely invalid because this person did not endorse any symptoms at all in the post & 3 month testing. Most people even outside of therapy report a few minor symptoms.

Taken together, the SCL 90R's results are very positive for Theophostic. They are the types of outcomes that build a logical case that Theophostic may indeed reduce emotional distress. The fact that 81% of participants had a reliable positive change (either Recovered or Improved) at post treatment and that many of these clients maintained their gains is encouraging. The number of cases (1) that reflect a negative outcome is also consistent with research on other psychotherapy approaches.

The Drop Out Rate

As happens in almost all clinical research, some clients dropped out of the study (six). This meant that 22 people started the study and 73% (N = 16) completed treatment. This dropout rate is similar to what occurs in much clinical research on individual psychotherapy, though we were surpised that our dropout rate was so comparable. Why? Because in grant-funded university investigations, clients are normally paid or given other positive incentives to stay in the study. Those of you who have had outpatient therapy before know that the therapist doesn't pay you in the real world, you pay the therapist! Outpatient clients in our study either used insurance and paid the deductible, or they paid out-of-pocket. Only those seeing lay counselors were seen for free. Considering the real world nature of this particular study, the drop out rate was very good.

Dysfunctional Attitude Scale (DAS) Results

What about TPM's premise that it reduces lie-based thinking? Researchers recently have provided recommendations on where functional people (in this case, people not seeking clinical treatment) score on the DAS.[10] However, we don't have a large sample of DAS scores from people who are in outpatient treatment to compare this with. This means we can't calculate clinical significance in the same manner as was done with the SCL- 90R. Fortunately however, there is an alternative strategy available, which we shall use.[11]

The score range for the DAS is 40-280, with lower scores reflecting more healthy beliefs. The initial average score for the current clinical sample was 144, with a standard deviation of 31. However, there was a clear bi-modal distribution in the sample. That means the score distribution looked like a camel with two humps. One hump represented four people in our sample who were already scoring in what previous research has suggested is clearly the normal range for this instrument (115 +/- 27)[12] and the other hump represented clients who were in a range of more clinical concern.

Okay, stay with me here. You can do this! The four participants who scored well-into the normal functional range were eliminated from the analysis since they were already very normal at the beginning (They had no place to improve to.) and they remained at that normal level throughout the study. That left us with eleven clients with more elevated DAS scores. The average and standard deviation for these clients of concern was 164 +/- 24. This became our key information to calculate the amount of change necessary to reflect the Improvement and Recovery levels of clinical significance.

Some clinical significance researchers suggest that one can define Improvement as one standard deviation's worth of change in the healthy direction, and Recovery as two standard deviations of change, provided that measurement error calculations (statisticians call this the Reliability Change Index) confirm this as appropriate. Applying the above to the remaining portion of the sample, the Improvement cutoff score would be ≤133 and the Recovery cutoff score would be ≤106. You can see that 106 is lower than the average of 115 for normal range populations, so this suggests we are on track logically. Table 3 highlights the DAS scores needed for all the clinical significance categories.

Table 3

Clinical Significance Cut-Off Scores for the DAS

Recovery	Reliable Improvement	No Reliable Change	Deterioration
≤106	≤133	>133	≥214

There, now that wasn't so bad, was it? Let's take a look at the individual clients for the entire sample and see how they fared. The four clients who started well within the normal range and maintained this range throughout the study were classified as Normal in terms of their beliefs. Remember that the score range for the DAS is 40 to 280, with lower scores reflecting fewer dysfunctional beliefs (better health). Also, the average for the normal population is 115 (Standard Deviation = +/-27). Clients are in the same order as they were for Table 2.

Table 4

Pretreatment, Post-treatment and 3-Month Follow-up DAS Scores

Client	Group	Pre	Post	Outcome	3 Month	3 Month Outcome
1	Outpatient	150	90	Recovered	105	Recovered
2	Outpatient	158	90	Recovered	86	Recovered
3	Outpatient	194	113	Improved	94	Recovered
4	Outpatient	180	121	Improved	141	No change
5	Outpatient	211	116	Improved	81	Recovered
6	Outpatient	120	108	Healthy	118	Healthy
7	Outpatient	171	66	Recovered	41	Recovered
8	Outpatient	U/A	U/A	U/A		
9	Outpatient	169	174	Unchanged	149	Unchanged
10	Outpatient	144	103	Recovered	106	Recovered
11	Outpatient	72	56	Normal	46	Normal
12	Outpatient	152	85	Recovered	100	Recovered
13	Outpatient	147	137	Unchanged	110	Improved
14	Lay	109	91	Normal	110	Normal
15	Lay	103	87	Normal	87	Normal
16	Lay	91	88	Normal	49	Normal

U/A = unavailable. This client did not complete the DAS. Perhaps the DAS was not included accidentally in the client's testing packets.

Now, let's take a better look at the summary data for our clients scoring in the clinical range on the DAS.

Table 5

Dysfunctional Attitude Scale Findings (N = 11)

Time of Testing	Recovery	Improvement	Unchanged	Deterioration
Post Treatment	6	3	2	0
3 Month Follow-Up	7	1	3	0

The above findings support Ed Smith's contention that TPM reduces lie-based thinking. Fifty four percent of these participants achieved Recovery status and another 27% reflected Improvement at post-treatment, making a total of 81% who reflected meaningful improvement. Only one client failed to maintain his gains at the three-month follow-up, none deteriorated, and a couple of clients improved further to the Recovered status. Taken together, the results support the logic that something good in the area of lie-based thinking has happened to most of these TPM clients.

The Religious Orientation Scale-Revised (ROS-R)

We also learn when an instrument doesn't yield clear-cut answers. The ROS-R was the only instrument that showed all participants' scores changing within measurement error (no significant change either way). What does this mean? One potential explanation is that the constructs measured by this instrument (intrinsic and extrinsic religious motivation) are stable trait-like conditions that are not changed through alterations in lie-based thinking. Another possibility is that the ROS-R lacks sufficient instrument sensitivity to be used with the types of people who show up for outpatient or lay counseling treatment (remember, the ROS-R only has data on non-clinical groups.). Other explanations are possible as well, so we really can't tell for sure. More research using the ROS-R instrument with people in psychotherapy treatment may one day help us figure this finding out.

The Spiritual Well-Being Scale (SWBS)

Reliable norms have yet to be established for the SWBS and some factorial difficulties have been identified;[13,14] therefore, clinical significance was not investigated in this particular instrument. What we can do is report the amount of change each client showed in the table below. One can readily see, like in the case of the DAS, that there was a bimodal distribution, with some clients starting treatment endorsing a high level of spiritual well-being and others not. To help in the interpretation of the results, we also included the average item score for the test in the post-treatment and three-month follow-up information. Remember, the SWBS was made with each item having a scale of 1-6. The total test score ranges from 20-120. Higher total scores reflect greater spiritual well-being, and overall item averages of 5.0 or above reflect a high degree of spiritual well-being as measured by this instrument.

Table 6
Spiritual Well-Being Scale Results

Client Number	Pre-TPM Total Score	Post-TPM Total Score	Post-Avg Item Score	3-mth TPM Total Score	3-mth Avg Item Score
1	91	106	5.3	103	5.2
2	104	112	5.6	113	5.6
3	104	116	5.8	115	5.8
4	76	113	5.6	111	5.6
5	78	110	5.5	116	5.8
6	72	97	4.8	94	4.7
7	U/A	U/A	U/A	U/A	U/A
8	U/A	U/A	U/A	U/A	U/A
9	68	54	2.7	75	3.8
10	103	108	5.4	110	5.5
11	119	120	6.0	120	6.0
12	90	102	5.1	113	5.6
13	73	102	5.1	95	4.8
14	100	102	5.1	107	5.4
15	58	77	3.8	66	3.3
16	110	101	5.0	111	5.6

U/A = These clients were missing this data. Perhaps the SWBS was accidentally omitted from their testing packets.

Five out of six of those with scores of 78 or below appeared to increase in spiritual well-being by the end of treatment. Three out of six also generally appeared to maintain most of their gains in this area. Again, we have to be cautious because of the difficulty determining clinically significant findings with these numbers. The results appear to cautiously support an association of TPM treatment with improved spiritual well-being.

Client Satisfaction Inventory and Three-Month Follow-up Satisfaction Results

How did the clients rate their treatment? Table 7 presents, by frequency and percentage, client responses to 12 questions asked post-treatment concerning their satisfaction with treatment. Of the sixteen clients, 14 reported consistently high satisfaction levels on the 12 questions. Readers are referred to the Appendix to view the Client Satisfaction Inventory itself, as we've just included enough of the question in the table to give you a good idea of what was asked. For the different numbers, 1 = Not at all, 2 = Very little, rarely, 3 = Somewhat, average, 4 = Often, more than anticipated, and 5 = Very much, above what was anticipated. Some questions were worded in an opposite direction to keep people from just checking all 5's or all 1's.

Table 7

Client Satisfaction Inventory Results (n = 16)

Question:	N/A	1	2	3	4	5
					Response by Frequency and Percentage:	
1: …counselor really seemed to care					2 (12.5%)	14 (87.5%)
2: My…counselor… put me down		16* (100%)				
3: I would …come back for more TPM…if I needed it.				2 (12.5%)	2 (12.5%)	12 (75.0%)
4: I would recommend TPM…					3 (18.8%)	13 (81.2%)
5: …my counselor was competent					3 (18.8%)	13 (81.2%)
6: TPM damaged my Christian faith		15* (93.8%)		1 (6.2%)		
7: I felt able to tell my …counselor whenever I was having problems	1 (6.25%)		1 (6.2%)	1 (6.2%)	2 (12.5%)	11 (68.8%)
8: I feel much better now…				3 (18.8%)	1 (6.2%)	12 (75.0%)
9: Compared to different types of therapy…I found the TPM sessions to be more effective.	2 (12.5%)				4 (25.0%)	10 (62.5%)
10: People who know me say TPM has made a positive change in me	3 (18.8%)			2 (12.5%)	3 (18.75%)	8 (50.0%)
11: I feel I've grown in my relationship with God through TPM.	1 (6.25%)		1 (6.2%)		1 (6.25%)	13 (81.2%)
12: The help I got from TPM was below what I expected.		14* (87.5%)	1 (6.2%)	1 (6.25%)		

*These questions were worded in an opposite direction to the others; hence, a 1 is the most positive score regarding Theophostic, 2 the second most positive, etc.

Taken together, the above results reflect a high degree of satisfaction with TPM when well-trained prayer ministers administer it. Concerning a comparison with other forms of treatment, fourteen clients previously had different forms of therapy. They rated TPM very high in comparison (all 4's or 5's). Most clients felt they had grown in their relationship with God (87%), and only one felt the help received from TPM was somewhat below what s/he expected (7%). Very few negative ratings are seen.

We added a three-months post-treatment questionnaire midway through the study (See Appendix). Clients were asked on a 4-point scale to rate the maintenance or loss of therapeutic gains since treatment ended. They were also asked if their participation in church activities had changed, and whether TPM had been helpful or unhelpful in the process of forgiving people who had been hurtful in the past. Eight clients completed these forms. Of these, 62% stated they had maintained the gains made from TPM sessions, and the other 38% stated they partially maintained the gains made in TPM sessions. None stated they had lost "most" or "all" of their previous gains. In the important area of the forgiving an offender, 88% endorsed TPM as helpful or very helpful. Church activity levels remained the same for most, with one endorsing an increase in activity level, and there was variation in the amount of church activities per week. Some clients self-administered TPM since treatment ended, suggesting that the form of prayer had become a regular coping skill for them.

Independent Reviewer Results

So the testing results were positive overall and most clients believed they had gained from experiencing TPM. The practitioner ratings of client improvement on the Brief Psychiatric Rating Scale also reflected positive changes. But what about an objective outside opinion? Perhaps the participants just got excited because they were in a study, or maybe they didn't want to hurt the feelings of the treating counselor? Perhaps we as researchers were biased in how we interpreted the data? Independent reviews are commonly recommended as a safety check for these types of concerns. The client is more likely to be honest with such reviewers so a safety check emerges for any enthusiasm or negativity found in the researchers. As a reminder, to qualify as a reviewer, these licensed mental health professionals were not affiliated with the study in any way, they did not practice Theophostic, and they did not know what type of intervention was being used.

So what did the reviewers do? After interviewing the clients and viewing their testing results and clinical record, they rated symptom levels of each client's primary Axis I disorder (i.e., their primary condition being treated). Reviewers rated symptom levels using a Likert 1 – 5 rating system (See Appendix). They then gave their overall assessment of the case outcome, giving an overall rating that represented their impression of treatment efficacy. Table 8 outlines these results on the next page.

Table 8

Independent Reviewer Findings

Client	Pre-tx GAF	Post-tx GAF	Primary Condition Being Treated	Symptom Reduction Rating	Overall Assessment of Outcome
1	60	70	Depression	Much	Much Improvement
2	55	68	Adjustment	Much	Much Improvement
3	62	75	Anxiety	Much	Much Improvement
4	65	75	Depression	Much	Much Improvement
5	65	75	Anxiety	Much	Much Improvement
6	62	71	Depression	Much	Much Improvement
7	65	75	Adjustment	Moderate	Much Improvement
8	75	85	Adjustment	Moderate	Much Improvement
9	55	62	Depression	Moderate	Moderate Improve.
10	60	65	Adjustment	Moderate	Much Improvement
11	63	79	Anxiety	Much	Much Improvement
12	60	75	Anxiety	Much	Much Improvement
13	60	75	Depression	Much	Moderate Improve.
14	60	80	Depression	Moderate	Mild Improvement
15	60	80	Depression	Moderate	Moderate Improve.
16	60	89	Anxiety	Moderate	Mild Improvement

At the end of TPM treatment, nine of the clients (56%) were rated with the highest rating allowed for symptom reduction (Much Improvement), and seven clients (44%) were rated as having moderate symptom reductions. The overall outcomes assessment also was very positive. Eleven clients (69%) were classified as Much Improvement (the highest ranking), three (19%) as Moderate Improvement, and two clients (12%) as Mild Improvement. These results are consistent with the psychological testing, therapist ratings, and client satisfaction results. The reviewers clearly believed that clients had benefited from treatment.

But that's not all. After the study, all the reviewers expressed great interest in learning about what was done to treat these people. They believed whatever was happening in this research project was beneficial for these people and they wanted to consider how it might be pertinent to their own practice. That says a lot to us as investigators.

Limitations in Case Study Research Design

As I (Fernando) intonated in the Preface, we must be cautious in interpreting these research findings. There are always limitations in conducting research, especially in real world settings like outpatient clinics and church lay counseling settings. If we could have changed anything in our design, for example, we would have loved to have a baseline of two or more testing periods spaced out over a month for each client prior to beginning treatment. Ethically, this would have been difficult since these were actual clients approaching the clinic/lay counseling center in distress, paying for treatment at the clinic, and wanting treatment right away. We also would have loved to have the Independent Assessors evaluate each client at the beginning of the treatment as well as the ending. That would have permitted a more precise evaluation of independently confirmed change. The training level of the clinicians and lay counselors involved was also important in limiting these findings. These clinicians and lay counselors were all well-trained in TPM and practiced within their competency level. Finally, we must remember the design limitations inherent in outcomes-based case study research projects themselves (on TPM or any therapy strategy, for that matter). The possibility of other factors besides the intervention (TPM in this case) leading to positive outcomes must be acknowledged in these designs. For example, perhaps these clients benefited because of the excellent personal characteristics of the clinicians and lay counselors. If other prayer ministers without these characteristics were used, perhaps the results might have been different. Randomized comparative or control group studies would be needed to control for these and other factors. Our case studies strongly support the need for such studies.

Summary of Case Study Findings

When we started this journey, I (Fernando) told you that I believed the numbers would speak for themselves in the end. Have they? Yes. From a researcher's perspective, they indicated that most of the people completing treatment in this preliminary study reported a positive outcome. This outcome was substantiated by testing, client satisfaction measures, therapist ratings, and an objective third party evaluation. The number of cases with improvement supports the logic that TPM had something to do with the outcome.

Some of you already picked up that I said "had something to do with the outcome" but I didn't say TPM "caused" these results or was proven effective. You're getting good! Yes, I have returned to the land of "science-speak" akin to the politicians. But remember, we scientists speak in this way for very different reasons than politicians. The research team now has very clear preliminary results that show a correlation between Theophostic treatment for anxiety, depression, and adjustment issues and symptom reductions. The results demonstrate the merits of more expensive and elaborate research designs (randomized control group or comparative designs). Since clients may need other interventions besides TPM alone, we recommend researching a counseling strategy plus TPM compared to that same strategy without TPM.

How does one address then the negative TPM stories (though fewer in number) that we as a research team have heard from some people outside this study? In our own study, only one client showed meaningful symptom elevations on the SCL 90R at the end of treatment. This preliminary finding is quite consistent with the percentage of negative outcomes reported on other more well-researched psychotherapies. What may be causing bad outcomes in other limited instances? While as researchers we could theorize about this matter, we chose to start generating ideas by interviewing Ed Smith himself (see the next chapter). In the future, mixed design qualitative research that includes people having both positive and negative experiences with TPM can then explore Smith's ideas. Our interview also includes other common questions therapists have about TPM. As more experimental and mixed design qualitative studies are done, both the positive and negative outcomes with TPM can be more fully understood. We are cautiously optimistic that TPM will eventually be found to be useful for symptom reductions in a variety of types of clients.

About Fernando Garzon, Psy.D.

Dr. Fernando Garzon is an Associate Professor in the Center for Counseling and Family Studies at Liberty University. He has a Psy.D. in Clinical Psychology from Fuller Theological Seminary and a B.A. in Biology from Wake Forest University. His interest areas include spiritual interventions in psychotherapy and Christian counselor education. Liberty University does not officially endorse Theophostic Prayer Ministry but rather supports the theological and scientific examination of this and other Christian intervention strategies. Correspondence regarding this book may be sent to Dr. Garzon at Liberty University, 1971 University Blvd., Lynchburg, VA 24502 or fgarzon@liberty.edu.

About Marian Teske, Psy.D.

Dr. Marian Teske received her Doctor of Psychology degree in clinical psychology from Minnesota School of Professional Psychology. She is a clinical psychologist working at Pathways Psychological Services in Elk River, MN.

About David Kleinschuster, Psy.D.

Dr. David Kleinschuster received his Doctor of Psycholoty degree in clinical psychology from Regent University. He is in private practice in Elizabeth City, NC

Chapter Six References

1. Jacobson, N.S., & Truax, P. (1991). Clinical significance: A statistical approach to defining meaningful change in psychotherapy research. *Journal of Consulting and Clinical Psychology, 59,* (1), 12-19.
2. Wiger, D.E., & Solberg, K.B. (2001). *Tracking mental health outcomes: A therapist's guide to measuring client progress, analyzing data, and improving your practice.* John Wiley & Sons: New York, New York.
3. Derogatis, L.R., & Savitz, K.L. (2000). The SCL-90-R and Brief Symptom Inventory (BSI) in primary care. In, M.E. Maruish, (Ed.), *Handbook of psychological assessment in primary care.* Mahwah, NJ: Lawrence Erlbaum.
4. Ogles, B.M., Lambert, M.J., & Masters, K.S. (1996). *Assessing Outcome in Clinical Practice.* Boston, Massachusetts: Allyn & Bacon.
5. Wiger, D.E., & Solberg, K.B. (2001). *Tracking mental health outcomes: A therapist's guide to measuring client progress, analyzing data, and improving your practice.* John Wiley & Sons: New York, New York.

6. Lambert, M.J. & Bergin, A.E. (1994). The effectiveness of psychotherapy. In S.L. Garfield & A.E. Bergin (Eds.), *Handbook of psychotherapy and behavior change.* New York: Wiley.

7. Ogles, B.M., Lambert, M.J., & Masters, K.S. (1996). *Assessing Outcome in Clinical Practice.* Boston, Massachusetts: Allyn & Bacon.

8. Wiger, D.E., & Solberg, K.B. (2001). *Tracking mental health outcomes: A therapist's guide to measuring client progress, analyzing data, and improving your practice.* John Wiley & Sons: New York, New York.

9. Wiger, D.E., & Solberg, K.B. (2001). *Tracking mental health outcomes: A therapist's guide to measuring client progress, analyzing data, and improving your practice.* John Wiley & Sons: New York, New York.

10. Dozois, D., Colvin, R., & Brinker, J. (2003). Normative Data on Cognitive Measures o f Depression. *Journal of Consulting and Clinical Psychology,* 71, 71-80.

11. Jacobson, N.S., & Truax, P. (1991). Clinical significance: A statistical approach to defining meaningful change in psychotherapy research. *Journal of Consulting and Clinical Psychology, 59,* (1), 12-19.

12. Dozois, D., Colvin, R., & Brinker, J. (2003). Normative Data on Cognitive Measures of Depression. *Journal of Consulting and Clinical Psychology,* 71, 71-80.

13. Ledbetter, M. F., Smith, L. A., Fischer, J. D., Vosler-Hunter, W. L., & Chew, G. P. (1991). An evaluation of the construct validity of the spiritual well-being scale: A confirmatory factor analytic approach. *Journal of Psychology and Theology, 19,* 94-102.

14. Miller, G., Fleming, W., & Brown-Anderson, F. (1998). Spiritual well-being scale ethnic differences between Caucasian and African-Americans. *Journal of Psychology an Theology, 12,* 358-364.

Chapter 7

Common Questions Asked Concerning Theophostic Prayer Ministry

Ed Smith & Fernando Garzon

Dr. Garzon's comment:

The preliminary research my team has completed has generated positive findings. The results appear to fit my own experience with the prayer form in my work. The combination of good initial research results, good experiences in practice with the prayer form, and the awareness of the negative experiences of some people led me to interview Ed Smith. I wanted to find out his thoughts on using TPM in therapy and understanding any negative outcomes.

The importance of the interview is clear. I've seen some articles and websites from critics of TPM that focus primarily on Smith's early writings (1997-2000) and do not consider his latest works (2007 and later). We all grow and develop, including Ed Smith. An emphasis on early writings significantly distorts people's impressions of Ed Smith's current views regarding his approach. However, criticism (even based only on early writings) is a good thing, and should be welcomed. Smith appears to have done this.

Indeed, Smith has gone to great efforts to dialogue with his critics. For example, he has presented on his approach to several Christian mental health professional organizations. These include the *American Association of Christian Counselors* (AACC) and the *Christian Association for Psychological Studies* (CAPS). At these conferences, he has had opportunity to talk personally with professionals with concerns and to respond to their questions. In 2005, he gave a draft of his revised TPM basic training manual to two of his most vocal critics for their examination and discussion at the 2005 international conference of the Christian Association for Psychological Studies. Along with a representative from his ministry and a psychiatrist who uses TPM, a discussion of his approach occurred that examined his current views and any concerns. Smith also had a representative of *Christian Research Institute* (CRI) review his 2005 work. That ministry's findings on his ministry as a whole have been positive. These behaviors demonstrate Smith is a humble man open to feedback from open-minded critics.

The questions below were sent directly to Ed Smith for his response. What you see are his answers. Further elaboration on his responses can be found in his 2007 basic training manual, or from his website in the "Frequently Asked Questions" section.

1. Are you suggesting that therapists not use other interventions and just use Theophostic Prayer Ministry?

Not at all. I am not discrediting traditional therapy at any level. If what is used works, and is producing life transformation in people, this is the mutual goal. If what others are achieving through other forms of counseling/ministry is resulting in people honestly proclaiming freedom, perfect peace and genuine lasting life transformation where there was emotional duress and dysfunction, then I rejoice with them. However, what I was finding in my own counseling ministry before using Theophostic principles, was what I now call "tolerable recovery". People improved but I never saw lasting genuine transformation and peace where there was once deep pain and inner turmoil. This lack of results may have been merely a reflection on my own ineptness. However, as I evaluated the outcomes honestly, I did not see deep and lasting change. I did see some results in areas where people merely needed instruction in life issues (example: communication, parenting, financial, etc.) but where there was deep emotional pain any evidence of lasting transformation that I witnessed was miniscule.

This "tolerable recovery" I was seeing in people did reflect some improvement in the person's condition; however, it often required constant attention and effort plus a strong support base to be maintained. Often once treatment was over, many of the people who improved (tolerable recovery) found themselves slipping back into their former conditions. Relapse was a common experience of those who got better (tolerable recovery). However, what I am now seeing with the people with whom I minister, seems to be genuine life transformation. Evidence of lasting transformation can be seen in people who are still reporting the same level of resolve in their emotional pain as the day they initially found peace. These people are some with whom I had ministered to over a decade ago at the beginning of TPM. I am also seeing outward transformation in behavior as a result of this residing peace. This is not only true in my own work but I continually receive unsolicited letters and emails from people from all around the world giving the same testimonies of lives changed. I understand that this is not empirical evidence and only my own personal experience and that of others.

I would like to bring a little clarification about some of what I read in this book. For the most part what has been written is genuine Theophostic Prayer Ministry. However, there were a few places where procedure was not completely "by the book." Nevertheless, the essence of what was done was within acceptable parameters and guidelines. The primary place where I need to bring clarification has to do with the facilitator asking the Lord to do one thing or the other as it related to memory, feelings and dealing with blockage. In the current training in Theophostic Prayer the facilitator should never ask the Lord to surface a memory, remove a blockage or take the person to any memory or show the person where he may need to go. The current training recognizes the active participation of the free will of the person in the process. Blockages, an inability to move forward, find a memory or "feel" has nothing to do with anything but the person's own belief and choice. It is assumed people will arrive at the place they need to be when they make the choice to do so. This choice will be made when the belief that is contrary to doing so is identified and resolved with God's truth intervention. If Jesus (the Holy Spirit) ever took a person to a memory he would have to violate the person's will since the only reason that the person is not going where he needs to go is because of choice.

One more point of clarification. I am fully aware that it is the Holy Spirit that communicates truth in a ministry session and not the person of Jesus. I am aware that any visual of Christ one reports seeing is a word picture and not the living representation of Christ in the flesh. However, making a clear distinction in the Trinity is not easily done and most people relate to God through Jesus at the relational level of communication.

2. Do you believe medications are ever necessary to treat mental health-related diagnoses?

Yes. Theophostic *cannot* resolve true mental illness. If the emotional duress and consequential behaviors are rooted in the person's biochemistry and not lie-based, then Theophostic Prayer Ministry will have no impact in changing this specific condition since TPM deals with lies. If the reason for the emotional pain and troublesome behavior is genuinely biologically rooted, then that is a truth, not a lie. However, where there is a biochemical reason for the emotional status of a person, this may be treated with medication. Theophostic Prayer Ministry is focused on the lie-based thinking of the person that drives the symptomatic behaviors that need to be stopped. However, when conditions are a result of a combination of a biochemical imbalance and faulty thinking, Theophostic can help with the faulty thinking component of the equation. I assume that all people are lie-based at some level (whether chemically imbalanced or not) and need their minds renewed with truth since no one has perfect thinking. To the degree that ministry is focused here, there is potential for all people finding some level of improvement. Does this mean that everyone needs Theophostic Prayer? No. Theophostic Prayer is but one avenue that God appears to be using to accomplish mind renewal. However, all people need their minds renewed one way or the other.

3. Are you downplaying the role of sin as a potential root of someone's emotional problems?

No. I do not see ministry to people in emotional pain as an "either-or" situation when it comes to sin or lies. In most every case it is both. If I am deceived and my emotional pain is stirred, I will be prone to act out the pain. When I do this, I sin. When this is the case, I must deal with the sinful choices and behaviors through confession and restitution as needed. I must also deal with the lies in my mind where the pain is coming from and find renewing truth. As I do this I can walk in more consistent victory. If I only address the sin and never deal with the lies behind many of my sinful choices, I am doomed to a perpetual cycle of sin, confession, repentance, performance-based-spirituality and eventual defeat. Just because Theophostic Prayer Ministry does not place heavy emphasis on rooting out sin does not mean that it is not important. It is assumed that people understand the necessity of dealing with sin since this is a primary focus of many churches and ministries. Theophostic Prayer Ministry is primarily focused on lies but deals with sin when sin is indeed that which is the presenting concern. It is a misunderstanding to assume that since Theophostic Prayer Ministry has not included all aspects of the teachings of the Church, that these teachings are not important or valid. In the same way that an evangelism program focuses on winning souls and does not deal with other aspects of the Christian life, so to Theophostic Prayer Ministry has as its focus identifying lies that are causing people life difficulty but fully acknowledges the importance of dealing with sin. Theophostic Prayer does not teach about taking communion, reaching the lost for Christ or Scripture memorization but these are all important just not the focus of this ministry.

4. Can Theophostic Prayer Ministry cause negative outcomes such as False Memory Syndrome?

First the term "false memory" is not a psychological term and in fact a false memory can not even exist as a memory. The term "false memory" is an oxymoron. If a memory is false then it is not a memory but rather a fabrication. It is true that some people do sometimes mistake a fabrication for a memory. I think this is very rare in the context of the tens of thousands of counseling sessions occurring daily around the country in a sundry of counseling and ministry settings. More often there is misinformation in a real memory. No memory is totally accurate in all detail thus allowing a real memory to contain misinformation. However, implanting a complete fabrication of an event that never occurred is rare and would require much effort on the therapist's part and a very submissive and willing recipient. The TPM process is very careful to avoid all possibility of this ever occurring. If it did occur then it would not be Theophostic Prayer being used just bad therapy. Here is where a counselor or ministry facilitator must handle loosely any memory that is reported until corroboration of other witnesses and documentation can be provided. At the same time, if no corroboration or documentation can be obtained this does not mean something did not occur.

Nevertheless, Theophostic Prayer "overkills" on avoiding falsehoods and fabrications from ever entering into the ministry session. First, Theophostic Prayer Ministry only deals with memory content that the person comes up with on their own without the help, suggestions or insinuations of the one doing ministry. Some have suggested that Theophostic Prayer Ministry places a person in a vulnerable suggestive state where the minister proceeds to implant false ideas. This is not the case at all in a true Theophostic session. The minister should never suggest anything during the process no matter how convinced he is in the validity of what he believes. Theophostic Prayer Ministry teaches the minister to get out of the way and refrain from all forms of suggesting or implanting. The minister should only ask questions that are reflective of the context of the information that the person has revealed. To say or ask something such as "I wonder if someone molested you?" or "You have symptoms of being molested as a child," or "I think you may be a satanic ritualistic abuse victim or a survivor of a government mind control project" are completely forbidden, out of line, and do not represent Theophostic Prayer Ministry in any form.

Theophostic Prayer Ministry does not lead a person to get into a relaxed or trance state any more so than any other typical ministry or counseling session. The person simply sits in his chair while he focuses on his present negative feelings. There is no counting backwards, thinking of a safe place; following the swinging pocket watch or any other regressive hypnotic approaches. The person is simply asked to feel and encouraged to discern what he feels and why he feels it. Theophostic Prayer Ministry avoids the use of hypnotic practices in any form. This is nothing really different here than what happens in meditative prayer or even a typical cognitive therapy session. When we pray we enter into a meditative mode of spiritual receptivity focusing on what God has for us. Theophostic Prayer Ministry is in its most basic form, simply prayer.

There are some misinformed people who mistakenly conclude that through Theophostic Prayer Ministry the minister/counselor is implanting false memories in the recipient's mind. They suggest this because some of the memories that surface were not consciously known before the session and do not believe that a person would forget a traumatic event. Experience has clearly demonstrated that memories can be repressed and often are. There is an abundance of evidence of documented cases of childhood abuse of which the person as an adult has no conscious memory. Which one of us remembers every aspect of our life? We remember parts and places but only selected events are actually consciously available at any given time. There is much evidence that repressed memory does in fact occur and is not uncommon.

(See http://www.brown.edu/Departments/Taubman_Center/Recovmem/other.html)

I am notorious for losing things. I lose my keys, glasses, and sometimes my car in the parking lot on a regular basis. Yet the truth is, these items are not really lost because somewhere in my mind the information exists that I need. The pertinent information that knows the location of the "lost" item is somewhere in my mind. The problem is that I cannot access this information. Here is how I know that I have this information in my mind. As soon as I find the lost item I will respond something like, "Oh, yeah, now I remember, that's where I left it." Finding the item surfaces the memory of having placed the item in that spot in the first place. It would be nice if I could just command this information to surface but I cannot. It has been stored outside of my conscious awareness. Similarly but more severely, if something happens to me as a child that I do not want to remember my mind can actually perform this same task. It can place this undesirable information in a place where I cannot consciously find it. I believe that this process of suppression is a survival tactic of my mind that God has equipped it to do. When my subconscious mind believes it is safe to release the information, as in a Theophostic session, it very well may release the traumatic memory.

5. You mention that TPM does not cause false memory "in a true ministry session." What are some signs that one is receiving a true ministry session versus something else that might lead to false memories?

First, the facilitator should not be guiding or directing the process. Second, the facilitator should be avoiding all forms of imagery or guided visualization. Third, the facilitator should not be giving the person truth or his opinions or thinking about what they believe is happening. If you are in the memory they should only be helping you to discern the lies and inviting Jesus to reveal His truth. If they are telling you what they think God wants you to know then they are not doing Theophostic Prayer Ministry. If they have a thought about what they think may have happened to you, they should never suggest it. In other words, the facilitator should avoid all forms of leading questions or statements or asking any questions that are asking for memory content. The facilitator should never be "filling in the blanks" in a memory story line. Please read through the printed sheet entitled "Theophostic Prayer Ministry Session Guidelines" that can be obtained from our website www.theophostic.com. These guidelines are a summary of what should happen in a Theophostic session. Every effort is made to keep implantation of thinking from ever occurring. I am not aware of any other counseling/ministry practice that has so many protective measures in place. A good over riding principle is this, "Anytime a ministry facilitator ever does anything to move the session in any direction that he thinks it should go he is no longer doing Theophostic Prayer."

6. Is Theophostic Prayer Ministry similar to or related to what is known as a "Repressed Memory Therapy"?

Theophostic Prayer Ministry is clearly not Repressed Memory Therapy (RMT) and denounces its practices. Though there is no doubt that inaccuracies do occasionally exist within the context of the many thousands of reported cases and allegations of abuse, it is inaccurate to assume that all recovered memory is thus inaccurate or invalid because of this rarity. It seems that some advocates of "false memory" want to declare all memories (not formerly conscious prior to counseling or ministry sessions) as fabricated and in question. It is obvious that verification for any reported memory is best achieved when collaboration by other witnesses can be obtained. However, the absence of collaboration does not invalidate what one remembers, it simply makes it more difficult to verify. The fact that there is collaboration in recovered memory of abuse both by outside witnesses and perpetrator's confessions makes it impossible to rule out the fact that repressed traumatic memory does exist. On the research website of Professor Ross E. Cheit of the Taubman Center for Public Policy & American Institutions at Brown University list over 100 court cases where repressed memory was a factor and corroborating evidence was used to verify its accuracy, so we know that it is a reality.

(See http://www.brown.edu/Departments/Taubman_Center/Recovmem/archive.html)

The challenge is not in determining the validity of its reality but rather in the validity of each individual case. This is something that we must seek to be diligent to do. We must avoid assuming that what is reported is absolute fact unless we have substantial collaboration. However, we cannot dismiss the authenticity of one's report simply because it cannot be verified with collaboration.

It seems today there is a more balanced perception emerging as these former techniques (RMT) are being laid aside by many practitioners and more careful approaches are being administered. The good news is, our society has lost its false innocence that allowed the evil presence of abuse to hide and has opened her eyes, facing this reality and thus approaching it with more caution and wisdom. Theophostic Prayer Ministry provides a very safe approach to accomplishing this. Let me restate myself, Theophostic Prayer Ministry has no commonalities with former approaches such as RMT. Theophostic Prayer Ministry is not only distinctly different it also denounces the principles advocated by RMT.

Even though repressed memory is believed to exist in some cases, such is not a primary focus in the Theophostic Prayer Ministry training. It is assumed by Theophostic Prayer Ministry that most memory dealt with during a ministry session will be that which has been consciously known prior to the ministry session. However, should repressed memory surface during a ministry session it should not occur as a result of the facilitator "digging" it up or implanting it. If this should ever occur then the facilitator is deliberately stepping outside the guidelines of this ministry approach and engaging in some other technique that is NOT Theophostic Prayer Ministry.

Memories are never completely accurate in every detail in any case. The very nature of how our minds record and assimilate information does not allow for this. Memory consists of the information that passes through the person's five senses at the time of the event, becomes mixed and interpreted by other memory experiences and eventually changes and fluctuates over time. My memory recall is not a video play back but rather an assimilation of many factors. Does this invalidate memory? If so, then open the prison doors of all those who where sent there by eye witness testimony. However, inaccuracies in details in a memory do not invalidate the experience itself. Just because I cannot remember the time and place or even the person who hurt me, does not mean that I was not hurt. However, this reality does demand a careful handling of memories that surface in a counseling/ministry session whether repressed or conscious. The same argument that suggests that all repressed memories are fabricated, can be used to discredit conscious memory as well. How do I prove that I saw a bald eagle on my nature hike if I was the only one on the trail?

There are also studies that have suggested children can be lead to believe details that supposedly occurred when in reality they did not. For example, it is possible to suggest a falsehood about some detail concerning a weekend trip little Johnny made to a theme park. One can ask little Johnny if he saw Bozo the Clown at the Theme Park and he may agree even though in reality he actually only saw Smiley the Clown. This does not constitute a false memory since Johnny did go to the theme park and he did see a clown, it just was not Bozo. The falsehood is not in whether the event ever occurred but rather the details in the memory. This would not be a false memory but rather a true memory containing misinformation. This is where collaboration is important in sorting out details in any memory. However, convincing a little child that they saw Bozo rather than Smiley is a far cry from convincing a child that he had been raped. There was a study done with college students who were asked to write out a report concerning a national tragedy they had recently witnessed on a news report. Years later when they were asked to report again on the same event and it was noted that their memory had changed from their initial report. This suggested that memory does change over time. Nevertheless, in both reports the essence of national tragedy was still in their memory even though the details had faded. The fact remained that the tragedy had occurred but the details recalled had fluctuated. A memory should be assumed invalid only when the particular event itself is determined to be false not just because some aspects of the event have fluctuated. If I cannot recall exactly who it was that hurt me does not mean that I was never hurt. Arriving at the accuracy of details is very important but the absence does not invalidate that something has happened. This is especially important when the details pertain to identities of perpetrators. We must be slow to declare someone's guilt and confront only when we can do so in the peace of Christ and with genuine compassion. This requires the victim find true healing and freedom.

Theophostic Prayer Ministry seeks to reach a place of perfect peace in the memory, genuine compassion and forgiveness for those who have hurt us and obvious life transformation. It is not about confrontation, retaliation or vengeance. However, it is about truth. If the truth is, someone that I needed to be able to trust proved untrustworthy then this is the truth. Therefore this relationship can never be mutually reciprocated in love until the one who has violated such trust come clean and be fully responsible for their choices. Until then, I can have compassion, pray for and offer the forgiveness of Christ but I cannot have a relationship beyond this point.

7. Given the detail of your response, could you give us a clear comparison of what happens in Repressed Memory Therapy versus what happens in a Theophostic Prayer Ministry session?

Each basic technique of Recovered Memory Therapy is listed below and followed a comparative review of Theophostic Prayer Ministry

- **Recovered Memory Therapy sometimes uses check-off lists of symptoms.** Recovered Memory Therapy sometimes uses a "check off" list of questions that are believed to be symptoms that indicate the presence of repressed memory. For example: Do you have an aversion to sex? Do you feel uncomfortable to enclosed places? Do you have a fear of water? Does the number 666 bother you?

- **Theophostic Prayer Ministry does NOT incorporate any symptoms "check-off" list.** People are rather asked to identify the emotional pain in their life and seek to discover its source. The source is usually discovered to be a false belief that was learned in a real life experience and now seated in a consciously held memory. This is very similar to the practices of typical cognitive approaches to counseling.

- **Recovered Memory Therapy suggests that recovering repressed memory is essential to symptomatic improvement.** Some resources say that the Recovered Memory Therapist operates under the assumption that ALL symptoms are indicative of repression.

- **Theophostic Prayer Ministry does believe that painful emotions, dysfunctional behavior and most disorders (eating, personality, etc) do have sources that are rooted in faulty thinking.** *Theophostic Prayer Ministry assumes that "bad symptoms" are generally connected to "bad thinking" whether repressed or conscious.* It is probable that *some* of the faulty thinking a person may have may be rooted in repressed memory. To the degree that this is true, logic would say that this faulty thinking needs to be exposed and replaced with truth before the consequential symptomology can be changed. Theophostic does not believe that recovering repressed memory is essential to symptomatic improvement but rather that exposure of lies and their displacement with truth is essential whether the memory be repressed or conscious. Theophostic Prayer Ministry does not teach that merely uncovering memory will result in any change whatsoever. It is very possible that the uncovering of painful memory will intensify the person's emotional duress rather than resolve it. Theophostic Prayer Ministry teaches that it is not the event itself that is sustaining the negative painful emotion but rather the lie-based interpretations contained in the memory. Therefore merely uncovering the event alone will have no real impact on reducing the discomfort.

- **Recovered Memory Therapy opponents suggest that the soil needed for the implantation of "false memory" is cultivated in the context of group therapy.** This is believed to happen as therapist mix people who have reported "repressed memory" with new group members who have not yet "come into" the knowledge of their supposed repression. It is here that they are indoctrinated with abuse stories and memory content that they naively are lead to embrace as their own.

- **Theophostic Prayer Ministry does not advocate the use of group therapy when administering this ministry process.** This is not to say that group therapy does not have value in its proper context. Nevertheless, Theophostic Prayer Ministry is prayer that is focused on an individuals specific lie-based issue with a goal of having a personal encounter with the presence of Christ. Theophostic Prayer Ministry does not teach the necessity of group dynamics or support around an issue or personal struggle. Theophostic Prayer Ministry does not teach a necessity for discussing historical emotional wounds in a group setting. Theophostic Prayer Ministry encourages a person to embrace the emotional pain they are carrying and seek to find its lie-based cause.

- **Recovered Memory Therapy utilizes age regression techniques.** These techniques tend to be hypnotic in nature. For example the therapist might ask the person to envision himself entering into an elevator and lowering down floor by floor which represent regressing to earlier childhood ages. The lower he goes the younger he will become. The purpose is to uncover the repressed memories stored in these earlier childhood places.

- **Theophostic views this practice as poor therapy and denounces all techniques such as this.** There is no teaching in Theophostic Prayer Ministry suggesting that a person create any imagery to be used as a vehicle for time travel. However, one of the basic principles of Theophostic Prayer Ministry is the belief that *"my present emotional pain is not solely rooted in my present circumstance."* It is acknowledged that the present moment may contribute to my emotional distresses but this is not always the case. It is believed that emotional responses that surface from day to day are often rooted in unresolved lie-based memories (conscious and repressed) that are triggered by similar events in the present tense. For example, a woman who has a painful emotional reaction (example: panic attack) to her husbands sexual advances may be "triggered" emotionally by something that she believes about sex that is contained in a historical real life event. This does not mean she has repressed memory but it is a possible indication that she is holding onto some falsehood that is triggered by his sexual advances. This is not to say that her panic attacks could not also be rooted in her view of her present relationship to her husband. It is just as possible that it is a mixture of both. Negative emotion that is aroused in a present situation can be an "emotional trail" leading one back to its lie-based source. This is especially true for people who have ongoing painful symptoms that resonates on a daily basis. It is important to note that all cognitive activity is rooted in memory since everything apart from the present moment is past tense and thus only known by memory recall at some level. Therefore logic says that we have no other option but deal with memory no matter what form of counseling/ministry in which we choose to engage. From this perspective, anytime we deal with anything apart from the exact present moment (which is literally impossible to do), this becomes a form of "age regression" whether it be early childhood memory or memory of last week. For me to focus on what happened yesterday is to "age regress" to that time in my life. Theophostic Prayer Ministry believes that is presenting emotion is often connected to the memory containing the false belief which is the actual cause of this corresponding painful emotion. Theophostic teaches how to embrace the painful emotion and allow it to connect the person to its lie-based memory source. This is really no different that when a person hears an old song on the radio and suddenly feels sadness. It is very likely that if this person were to focus on the sadness and allow themselves to connect to its cause they would find themselves in a memory where they were made to feel sad in the context of this song being played.

- **Recovered Memory Therapy sometimes uses trance writing or "inner child" journaling.** Sometimes this is done while using hypnosis. The person is given a pen and encouraged to allow his or her supposed "inner child" to draw and express hidden memories and feelings. From these images it is concluded that there is repressed memory.

- **Theophostic Prayer Ministry does not advocate any practices such as this.** There is no encouragement for a person to get in touch with his or her inner child. There is no use of hypnosis. Journaling is not advocated or taught though there may be value for this in its proper context. However, the person is encouraged to learn to listen to themselves and to what they are really thinking and saying to themselves. What we say to ourselves can help us to discover what we believe that is producing the emotional distresses in our lives.

- **Recovery Memory Therapy sometimes uses body massage to release hidden memory.** A therapist massages places in the body where it is believed that cells have stored the memory of a particular trauma, releasing it to the brain to be remembered.

- **Theophostic Prayer Ministry does not use, advocate or encourage any form of massage therapy.**

- **Recovery Memory Therapy utilizes dream interpretation.** This practice is often found in the context of hypnotherapy. The person may be hypnotized and then asked to replay the dream where the therapist offers interpretation as it relates to possible repressed trauma and abuse.

- **Theophostic Prayer Ministry strongly discourages any interpretation of dreams, visual images, inner thoughts etc that might provide the recipient with false information.** The facilitator is taught to avoid all personal input as to any aspect of a person's memory content. Only that which the person surfaces on their own is dealt with and only to the degree that it reflects the specific context of the persons reporting. For a more detail description of this read the TPM Guidelines.

- **Recovered Memory Therapy sometimes uses drugs such as sodium amatol to aid in memory recovery.** This is a barbiturate drug (truth serum), that produces an altered state of deep relaxation. The therapist will engage in a "questioning" about the persons past using age regression techniques looking for assumed suppressed memories.

- **Theophostic Prayer Ministry NEVER uses any drugs in any form for any purpose.**

- **Recovered Memory Therapy may use "Spirit Guides" to help the person to discover their repressed memory.** The person is asked to envision a pathway looking for their personal guide into the hidden places in their mind. At some point the person may report a "Spirit Guide" who may even say he is Jesus. This guide is to aid them by revealing hidden "truths" about the past.

- **Theophostic Prayer Ministry views this practice as total deception and demonically driven.** Any such Spirit Guides would be identified as an evil impersonators of good that will ultimately lead the person into deception. Any "jesus" that might be encountered while engaging in this practice would be identified as demonic and rejected. This practice would be put in the same category as channeling and thus totally denounced by Theophostic Prayer Ministry.

- **Recovered Memory Therapy uses relaxation therapy techniques.** The therapist may have the person visualize a quiet safe place where they can let down their defenses and relax. It is while in this relaxed and suggestible state that the therapist may make memory suggestions.

- **Theophostic Prayer Ministry does not engage the person in any form of relaxation therapy.** The person is NEVER told to visualize anything or imagine being in any place other than the chair in which he or she is seated. The person is not told to relax or calm down or seek a place in their mind that is peaceful. To the contrary, the person is encouraged to focus on their absence of peace (if this is the case) and move toward the place in their thinking that is causing the discomfort. They are encouraged to feel the painful emotions not find a place to escape it in their mind. Theophostic Prayer Ministry is prayer. The person is asked to close his eyes if he or she desires to, and focus on the pain that they have brought with them into the session and then wait for what God has for them. Those who are opposed to prayer or unfamiliar with its elements might confuse this with some other form of treatment. Theophostic Prayer Ministry is unapologetic about being focused prayer. Some might suggest that since Theophostic Prayer Ministry has the person to close their eyes (optional and only suggested to allow them to focus on what they are feeling and thinking) that this is a form of hypnosis or relaxation technique. If this is the case then all religions including Christianity are guilty of practicing hypnosis since they are praying in like fashion. We are called to prayer in the Bible and told to own what we feel. For example we are commanded to "cast all of our anxiety upon Him (Jesus)." How can we do this with out owning it, feeling it and then choosing to cast it upon Him? Theophostic Prayer Ministry is about doing this. Theophostic Prayer Ministry teaches that it is possible and important to know why we are anxious (what we believe) as we choose to cast it onto the Lord.

8. Many of us have concerns about lay counselors working with people who have complex conditions—Dissociative Identity, substance abuse, eating disorders, suicidal clients, etc. What are your recommendations in this regard?

First of all, every member of the Body of Christ has been called to pray and minister. This is not to say that all members need to be dealing with complex issues people bring to a ministry session. Lay ministers should never be doing the role of a mental health professional but only prayer. Theophostic Prayer is not about counseling, diagnosing, offering advice or prescribing medication; it is about prayer. That is not to say that some lay ministers can be trained to do highly effective prayer work with complex issues. Nevertheless, the prayer facilitator should not be trying to treat any mental disorder but should rather only help the person identify the lies he or she believes. If an individual has a personality disorder that is organically derived the prayer minister can still do prayer ministry to address the lie-based thinking this person will also have. There is always the possibility the personality disorder may improve by the person reaching a deeper level of peace. Nevertheless, symptom reduction is not the focus or the goal of Theophostic Prayer even though it is often an outcome.

In our training, we instruct lay ministers to keep within their training experience and level of abilities, as should the mental health professional. In other words, you should know when you're in over your head. He/she should refer to a mental health professional, preferably trained in Theophostic, in such cases. We encourage them to maintain a consultative or supervisory relationship with a licensed therapist trained in TPM whenever possible. At the same time there is good anecdotal evidence that many lay ministers are providing valuable and credible ministry to people with complex issues while not doing counseling or psychotherapy. One should never assume that a credential necessarily equals efficacy. Theophostic Prayer Ministry trains a person to minister (not diagnose, counsel, or do therapy) with lie-based issues at all levels. As believers in Christ we are called by God to pray and minister to all people in all situations. It is important to know the difference between ministry and psychoanalysis.

Of course, it is preferable for someone with a complex condition to see a qualified licensed clinician trained in TPM than a lay minister whenever possible or at least the lay person should be working with the professional when dealing with complex issues if at all possible. This also assumes the person seeking ministry has good insurance and can also afford to do this. Many people have poor insurance or none at all, which leaves them with only the state system as an option outside of a lay minister. It is not likely that the professional mental health community is going to take on all the many hurting people who cannot afford services therefore the lay ministry is the next wave of defense. I believe our focus needs to be on equipping this willing army of ministers to be as effective as possible. Ideally, a strong network between mental health professionals and lay ministers can be established in the Theophostic community that could provide quality ministry from both worlds.

9. If a therapist uses Theophostic Prayer Ministry in clinical treatment, what are some general principles s/he should follow?

As with any intervention, therapists should do a proper assessment of the client and obtain informed consent. There are a few important questions regarding the client to consider. Is the client a Christian and open to Theophostic Prayer Ministry? Does the client have a condition appropriate to Theophostic (based on faulty thinking as a major component)? Of course, the therapist should have adequate training to administer Theophostic as well.

Informed consent needs to be written out (like with other significant interventions). The client should understand the prayer form sufficiently to evaluate the pros and cons of experiencing it. The prayer form may generate strong emotions and the surfacing of painful or repressed memories. Since research is at an early stage, this should also be known. Alternative treatments, some of which may have more research support, should be discussed. Like most interventions, you should also keep informed consent as both a decision in the beginning of using TPM and a process, checking every few Theophostic sessions with the client about their experience with the prayer form. Finally, the therapist should continue getting training in Theophostic. The mental health professional should also know what his state allows as far as a prayer-based approach to counseling.

10. What is your stance on doing research on Theophostic?

I welcome scientific studies on Theophostic. When I started this ministry, I didn't realize how important it was for some to have such research when I first began to train others using this ministry approach. Honestly, having the research will not have any real impact on me in that I am already convinced that God is doing mighty and wonderful things. The testimony of the tens of thousands of people worldwide is proof for me. The same test that we as the Church uses to determine the authenticity of a persons salvation is the same that I use to test the validity of this ministry. We choose to believe the "word of their testimony" and whether their fruit remains. If people show evidence that transformation has occurred and are walking in a deeper relationship with God something has happened. We did a survey some time ago with 150 pastors who were using TPM in their church ministry. There were many questions asked but three in particular are relevant here, "100% of those surveyed said that they recommend TPM to others, 98% of the pastors said they personally benefited from it, 96% found highly effective outcomes, 90% reported life transformation in the people who had received ministry." These are astounding findings. If 90% of the people with whom we offer ministry show life transformation we should jump for joy.

My own heart change and life transformation is proof to me (and to my wife and kids.) I am surrounded by others who also practice these principles as a spiritual discipline in their Christian lives and all are reporting lasting fruit. Nevertheless, I would be glad to collaborate with researchers to make sure they're administering the approach correctly in their studies. At the same time, I would not discount the testimonies of changed lives through Theophostic Prayer Ministry. I've seen too many of them, and many others using Theophostic have seen the same to just disregard TPM because it doesn't have much research yet. Therapists have used other psychotherapeutic approaches before the research on them came out. Let's do the research but not discount changed lives, either.

11. This research is positive and encouraging, and most personal testimonies we've heard are good about Theophostic Prayer Ministry. How do you explain some of the bad experiences we've heard of in addition to the good ones?

First of all, we need to look at the numbers. One should compare just how much negative is actually being reported as opposed to the positive? Just a cursory search on the Internet will provide some insight to this question. The last time I checked, there were only a few critics listed as compared to over 10,000 positive sites advocating Theophostic Prayer Ministry. It is important to also ask if a negative report should have any more weight than a positive. If not, then the positive far exceeds the minimal negative. A recent survey developed by a doctoral student (not associated with Theophostic Prayer Ministry) was given to over 2500 people who said they had received Theophostic Prayer indicated a very high satisfaction rating. The summary of this survey can be found on the TPM website at **www.theophostic.com**. We also must not forget that every avenue of helping care whether it be prayer ministry, cognitive therapy, psychoanalysis, or even in the medical arena have examples of things going bad. However, for the most part bad experiences are usually isolated cases and almost always reflect on the administrator of the practice and not the practice itself. I do not of any case where Theophostic Prayer is said to have gone bad where the person administering it was in fact administering TPM by the book. In every case that I have followed up on it was not TPM that was the problem but rather a facilitator doing something else but calling it TPM.

There are several things I believe can contribute to a bad experience with Theophostic:

- *What the practitioner calls Theophostic Prayer Ministry may not indeed be Theophostic Prayer Ministry.* Sometimes people take a little of what is taught in this approach and then mix it with other things. For example, some people might get directive ("Go to this memory", "Find a safe place in your mind", "Envision Jesus standing near by.") or they might not allow the person the freedom to slow down, go at their own pace, and deal with things when they are ready ("You have to face this painful memory now"), etc. These tactics violate Theophostic Prayer Ministry's basic principles of being non-directive and respectful for the individual to go at their own pace. It is important to place the

"Theophostic Prayer Ministry Session Guidelines" over the top of any experience to determine if what has occurred is actually in line with this Ministry Approach. I read a report about a bad experience that occurred in which Theophostic Prayer Ministry was blamed for the outcome. As I read what actually happened in the ministry session, it was clearly apparent that this was not a Theophostic Prayer Ministry session. What was actually being administered was guided imagery, the use of suggestive questioning, directive counseling and aspects of Recovered Memory Therapy. Before conclusions are drawn in any given scenario, it is important first to determine if genuine Theophostic Prayer Ministry is being employed or not.

- *Sometimes lack of preparation for the person to receive TPM is the problem.* People need to be aware of what the prayer form entails and that they might experience some strong emotions and painful memories. If the person is surprised by these and the prayer minister does not process the post-prayer experience well with the person, they might go away reluctant to try TPM again, even if the Lord did some wonderful healing in the experience.

- *Sometimes prayer ministers try to work with conditions that are beyond their level of training.* It is always important to know your limits and when to refer to another resource. Sometimes this can mean a licensed mental health professional (ideally trained in TPM). TPM discussion or supervision groups can be very useful in helping you recognize when you need to refer.

- *Ministry modalities and practices should not be judged based on the efficacy of the practitioner administering the process.* If a medical doctor is negligent in his practice by failing to maintain the standards and protocol of his profession, the medical school, which awarded him his degree, is not blamed or held accountable. The line of thinking that judges this ministry approach based on the outcomes of a few who practice the approach poorly is illogical and not the standard applied to other modalities of ministry.

- *Sometimes people become more emotionally unstable as a consequence of doing this ministry before they become noticeably better.* This is not uncommon in many forms of ministry, psychotherapy, and counseling. Actually, most regular psychotherapy informed consents have a statement included advising people of this possibility, whatever approach to therapy is being used. Why does this sometimes happen? People often have much pain blocked out and suppressed. When they initially come for help there is an uncovering and realization of the pain that might burst forth. This can be a very uncomfortable time. Some people might see this as a bad thing and withdraw from the ministry process and thus interpret their worsened state as failure on the part of the process. However, for those who are willing to press in and continue the ministry and find the root sources of the pain, transformation can occur. Here again, it is important to examine each situation for the details of what occurred that resulted in a negative report being made.

In summary several questions need to be asked in each situation before determining what is at the heart of the matter:

o   Does what happened in the ministry session match what is taught in the Theophostic Prayer Ministry process? Did the facilitator follow protocol and the stated guidelines? (almost always where there is a negative report, I believe some principle has been violated or guideline not followed.)

o   Was the facilitator working outside the parameters of his or her expertise or should there have been a referral made or the presence of supervision?

o   Was the recipient of ministry well informed as to the particulars of the ministry approach?

o   Was the facilitator ill equipped and ineffective in his or her administering the Theophostic Prayer Ministry process?

o   Did the recipient of ministry end the process before he or she had come to a place of emotional stability and well-being or did he or she end the process at the surfacing of emotional pain?

There will always be some measure of negative reporting in any field of ministry, psychotherapy, or counseling. The increasing numbers of lawsuits prevalent today does not seem to be coming from any one venue of counseling or ministry modality. People are reporting negative experiences across the board from all camps. The common denominator does not seem to be approach but rather a sundry of things. My theory is, ultimately, the primary factor will be found to be the individual doing ministry and not the form or process that he or she is practicing. Since this is my belief, we seek to equip people with as thorough understanding in this ministry process as possible. We seek to provide ongoing training and encouragement to better equip those doing ministry to be the best they can for the cause of Christ.

12. Does Theophostic Prayer Ministry provide any specific guidelines for those who are seeking this form of ministry to better assure that the client is getting what they are looking for?

There are several resources that a person can avail themselves of when seeking out a person who claims they are using Theophostic Prayer Ministry. These resources can be downloaded from the Theophostic website at www.theophostic.com under the heading "Seeking Personal Ministry." One is a questionnaire that the person can have the facilitator/counselor complete before the first session. Another is what we call our TPM Session Guidelines. This is a page or qualitative statements that clearly define what should happen in a Theophostic Prayer Ministry session. We strongly encourage all people who seek ministry to familiarize themselves with this sheet. A final resource is the book "Healing Life's Deepest Hurts." This is an overview and introduction to the basic principles of Theophostic Prayer Ministry.

Concluding Statement by Dr. Garzon

You've now seen the positive results of this preliminary investigation and heard directly from Ed Smith regarding questions about TPM. You also have a clear sense of the limitations to this case study research and where the research needs to head to answer questions about TPM. In doing this project, I (Fernando) have had the chance to interact with Dr. Smith, ask him some hard questions, and check the data myself to see if the numbers were stacking up. For an exploratory study, they certainly do. Experimental studies are clearly warranted on TPM. Aside from the project itself, I found Dr. Smith to be a humble, Godly man who was very receptive to my questions, concerns, and comments. This bodes well for Theophostic.

Appendix

Sample Forms Used in the Study

Instructions to the External Reviewer

Thank you for your willingness to help us evaluate the outcome of therapy with this client. You are playing a valuable role in our assessment of some therapy techniques we're researching. We would like you to do three things in your conversation with this client.

1. Help us assess whether the diagnoses the client came in with have been effectively treated. Are the symptoms of the disorders still present and, if so, to what degree?
2. Help us learn whether the client has experienced general improvements in his/her level of functioning and quality of life. Your completion of this brief questionnaire and any comments will be helpful in this regard.
3. Finally, we'd like to know how the client experienced the therapy. As you know, sometimes clients don't give therapists feedback (positive or negative) that would be helpful to know.

Again, thank you so much for your willingness to meet with this client for this review.

Sincerely,

Fernando Garzon, Psy.D.

External Reviewer Form

External Reviewer: _____
Case: _____
Date: _____

1. Axis I & II Diagnoses at treatment outset:

_____

_____

_____

GAF Score: _____

(Continued on next page)

2. Based on your interview with the client, as well as an examination of the clinical record, please rate the client's current symptom levels related to the above diagnoses:

Diagnosis 1, _____

1	2	3	4	5
Symptoms Worse	No change	Mild reduction in symptoms	Moderate reduction in symptoms	Much reduction in symptoms

Diagnosis 2, _____

1	2	3	4	5
Symptoms Worse	No change	Mild reduction in symptoms	Moderate reduction in symptoms	Much reduction in symptoms

Diagnosis 3, _____

1	2	3	4	5
Symptoms Worse	No change	Mild reduction in symptoms	Moderate reduction in symptoms	Much reduction in symptoms

3. Your estimate of a current GAF score: _____

4. Please rate your overall impression of treatment efficacy in regards to this client:

1	2	3	4	5
Client worsened	No improvement	Mild Improvement	Moderate improvement	Much improvement

5. Considering your total clinical experience with this particular population, how mentally ill is the patient at this time?

        1 Normal

        2 Borderline Mentally Ill

        3 Mildly Ill

        4 Moderately Ill

        5 Markedly Ill

        6 Severely Ill

        7 Among the most extremely ill patients

Comments:

Theophostic Client Satisfaction Inventory

This questionnaire is designed to measure the way you feel about the Theophostic ministry you have received. It is not a test, so there are no right or wrong answers. Answer each question by placing a number beside each one as follows:

1 = Not at all
2 = Very little, rarely
3 = Somewhat, average
4 = Often, More than anticipated
5 = Very much, above what was anticipated
X = Does not apply

1. _____ My Theophostic prayer counselor really seemed to care about me.
2. _____ My prayer counselor put me down when I disagreed with him/her.
3. _____ I would likely come back for more Theophostic ministry with my prayer counselor if I needed help again.
4. _____ I would recommend Theophostic ministry to people I care about.
5. _____ I felt my prayer counselor really knew what s/he was doing.
6. _____ Theophostic ministry damaged my Christian faith and walk.
7. _____ I felt able to tell my prayer counselor whenever I was having problems with the Theophostic prayer.
8. _____ I feel much better now than when I first came here.
9. _____ Compared to different types of therapy or ministry I've received, I found the Theophostic sessions to be more effective.
10. _____ People who know me say Theophostic Ministry has made a positive change in me.
11. _____ I feel I've grown in my relationship with God through Theophostic prayer.
12. _____ The help I got from Theophostic Ministry was below what I expected.

Theophostic Client Satisfaction Questions

1. Have you had therapy before without Theophostic? If so, how did Theophostic Ministry compare?

2. Please make any other comments you would like us to know about your experience with Theophostic. Feel free to write on the back of this paper if necessary.

Theophostic Three Month Client Questionnaire

1. Over the last 3 months since Theophostic Prayer Ministry, I believe that (please check one):

       ___I have maintained the gains made in Theophostic counseling.
       ___I have partially maintained the gains I made in Theophostic counseling.
       ___I have lost most of the gains made in Theophostic counseling
       ___I have lost all the gains made in Theophostic counseling

Comments:

2. Please evaluate Theophostic Prayer Ministry's helpfulness or lack of helpfulness in the process of forgiving people who had wounded you in the past.

       ___Theophostic was not helpful
       ___Theophostic was helpful
       ___Theophostic was very helpful
       ___Unable to evaluate

Comments

3. Since I received Theophostic Ministry, my participation in church-related activities (worship services, Sunday School, group Bible studies) has

       ___increased
       ___remained the same
       ___decreased

Comments:

4. I attend church, group Bible study, or other religious meetings

> ___three or more times a week
> ___twice a week
> ___once a week
> ___a few times a month
> ___major holidays
> ___rarely or never

5. I practice Theophostic ministry on myself (i.e., without anyone ministering to me)

> ___More than once a day
> ___Daily
> ___Two or more times/week
> ___Once a week
> ___A few times a month
> ___Rarely
> ___Never have done this

Comments:

Printed in the United States
111196LV00002B/251-1500/P